# NONSENSE on Stilts

# NONSENSE on Stilts

## THE GETTYSBURG ADDRESS & LINCOLN'S IMAGINARY NATION

### BY
### PAUL C. GRAHAM

SHOTWELL
COLUMBIA · So. Car.
Est. 2015
PUBLISHING

Produced in the Republic of South Carolina by

**SHOTWELL PUBLISHING LLC**

Post Office Box 2592

Columbia, So. Carolina 29202

**www.ShotwellPublishing.com**

Cover Design by Boo Jackson.

ISBN: 978-1-963506-02-0

FIRST EDITION

10 9 8 7 6 5 4 3 2 1

# CONTENTS

You need only reflect that one of the best ways to get yourself a reputation as a dangerous citizen these days is to go about repeating the very phrases which our founding fathers used in the struggle for independence.

— Charles A. Beard (1874 – 1948)

# PREFACE

**LIKE MY PREVIOUS WORK**, *CONFEDERAPHOBIA: An American Epidemic*, this little book started out as an article that garnered some attention when it was first written (2013). Some months back, well more like a year or so ago, I had to come up with a presentation for my local Sons of Confederate Veterans Camp.[1] I dusted off this one and modified it to be used as the basis of a presentation. It went over very well, and several people asked me to send them a copy of it. Having more or less forgotten the issue, the attention it drew gave me what I needed for the basis of this new publication. As I am writing this, the 160th anniversary of Lincoln's Gettysburg Address has just passed. In this book I jump off at the sesquicentennial of the address and this is fortunate. There was much, much more going on to illustrate this cultish tribute than at the most recent observance, although the commentary on the great speech is just more of the same ole one-nation-indivisible talk.

That's where I started, true, but the filling-out part, the fruits of which you hold in your hand, took me in many strange places, events about which I knew little or nothing (but should have). In many places, I am just as shocked as you are (I suspect) as the exploration of the question explained in the next paragraph.

---

1    Lt.Gen. Wade Hampton Camp No. 273, Columbia, SC. Greetings compatriots!

The issue I pursue in this book is a straight-forward and simple one: Were the words of Abraham Lincoln's famous 'Gettysburg Address' true; or to put it another way, does Lincoln's accounting of America's founding and purpose correspond to reality as far as it can be known and documented?

This is a tight focus which, dear reader, by necessity, excludes topics such as slavery[2] or other emotive 'triggers.' Not only is this issue outside of the parameters of this work, but inclusion would make a serious look at the arguments and evidence on this topic almost impossible. Hackles would go up and the name calling would begin. It is not that I care about name calling—although I would prefer *not* to be subject to such behaviour as a general rule—it is more that I want you to be able to clearly see what I am trying to show you in a solid place, mentally speaking, without too many knee-jerk reactions, so we can follow the arguments and textual evidence together as I meander through the material.

Being a partner in the quest on one hand, or a sceptical observer on the other can provide a similar experience. One should always be suspicious, but willing to learn. Trust, but require verification. That's the ideal, anyway.

I beg your pardon in advance for my writing 'eccentricities.' I write like I think and like I talk in most cases. Sometimes I have to reel myself back in on a tangent. Other times, I may use 'some language,' but I've cleaned it up as much as I can or am willing to do.

---

2    For a good look at that issue, I suggest *Forced into Glory: Lincoln's White Dream* by the late Lerone Bennett, Jr. (1928-2018) (Chicago: Johnson Publishing House, Inc., 2000).

Mr. Bennett was an African-American scholar, author, historian, and former executive editor of *Ebony Magazine*. His research is impeccable and, for the sake of our 'confederaphobic' readers, he cannot be said to be a Confederate sympathiser in any way, shape, or form.

He gets Abraham Lincoln, race, and slavery exactly right, although his portrayal of the Confederate States of America is less than flattering. I've also written a short article on this topic years ago called 'How the War was About Slavery,' if you want a quick read on that topic from a Southern perspective, i.e., mine, you can find it here: bit.ly/graham-about-slavery.

'Agreeing to disagree' (what civilised people do) at the end of any 'inquiry' is the rule, not the exception among us humans. This is true whether you are squabbling over football at a bar, or engaging a book on the Gettysburg Address. I may not convince you, but it is my sincere hope that you will come away with a broader perspective. I know I am not the same after researching and writing it.

Before we start, I am going to need to define the word NATION. I don't want there to be any confusion about what I mean by this.

By Nation, I mean a *State* like Germany, France, Lithuania or Angola. One thing. Not a federation of any kind, but rather a centralised, top-down form of government—a government that rules the entire geographical territory of the 'country' and supersedes all local authority (or seeks so to do). This form of government is a creature of the rise of the nation-state—the government of post-revolution France, being one example of this phenomenon—with the characteristic of being 'one and indivisible,' hostile to local institutions, organic communities, and folk ways that stray from national identity, and capable of growth and expansion (by means fair or foul) which have nothing to do with the people over which they benevolently rule.

So, buckle-up, friends, it's going to be a wild ride. Remember you proceed of your own free will and accord. I'm holding nothing back. Not-one-damn-thing.

You have been given due notice. I leave the rest to you.

Paul C. Graham

Old Saxe Gotha, South Carolina

09 December 2023

# INTRODUCTION

ON 19 NOVEMBER 1863, ABRAHAM LINCOLN delivered his most revered oration at the dedication of the *Soldiers' National Cemetery* at Gettysburg, Pennsylvania.[3] As a work of English prose, The Gettysburg Address has few equals in the American literary canon. Eloquent and succinct, it has inspired Americans with almost religious awe for generations. It is one of the few instances of American oratory that has achieved a status akin to holy writ. It has become a kind of Nicene Creed that defines American orthodoxy. It is what 'real Americans' believe about their historical origins, their foundational ideals, and their collective mission.

There was not a better display of this *quasi-religious* adoration of this most American of speeches, than the Sesquicentennial mark of the celebrated speech.

On the big day, the 13th of November in the year of our Lord 2,013, thousands gathered at the Soldiers' National Cemetery at Gettysburg, Pennsylvania, to remember, to commemorate, and to celebrate Abraham Lincoln's most beloved oration. Lincoln's address was hailed by the participants not only for its eloquence, but also

---

3    I am aware that there are several versions of the address and that it is a matter of dispute which version (if any of the versions now known to exist) was given at the dedication. We will assume that the version most commonly used—the one most quoted and collected—is sufficient for the purposes of this book. It is also the one most people know or have at least heard.

for its 'inspirational' qualities, qualities which invigorated 'national ideals' and provided Americans (including you and I, one supposes) a definition of 'what a nation should be.'

Keynote speaker James McPherson, the (in)famous Civil War historian and presiding high priest of the ceremony, praised Lincoln's oratorical achievement in which he claimed, among other things, that the Gettysburg Address 'weaved together themes of past, present, and future; continent, nation, and battlefield; and birth, death and rebirth.'

The event was preceded by a quasi-religious (didn't I already use that phrase?) orgy in the media of praise and adulation. Articles and editorials from news outlets across the fruited plains of America and beyond joined in the chorus in praise of Lincoln's address. One newspaper in Harrisburg, Pennsylvania, even apologised over an editorial written by a staff member in 1863 who was critical of Lincoln's address. *This despite the fact that the reporter was actually there.*[4]

Apparently the editorial staff of the 21st century thought themselves a better judge of Lincoln's creation myth—mystically summoned from I know not where—than the one on the scene who—like any other person of his time that knew even a scintilla of history as it related to America's origins and form of government—was *not* taken in by the pretty, albeit scandalous words.

Their reason for this 150-year-old retraction?

Well, the man who actually attended the event and heard the address from Lincoln's own lips—as you may have already guessed—was on the 'wrong side of history'! (I could spend hours on what is wrong with the notion of history having sides, but one hopes that such a statement is self-evidently crazy.)

---

4    See "Retraction for our 1863 editorial calling Gettysburg Address 'silly remarks'" by PennLive Editorial Board, *Patriot News,* (PennLive.com), 14 November 2013 (Accessed 02 December 2023). Quick Link: bit.ly/SillyRemarks1863.

If you think this kind of hindsight apology on the part of a newspaper is unique to the hysteria surrounding the sesquicentennial of the address, the handwringing continues. UK paper *The Guardian,* to give one example of many, apologised on 07 May 2021 for supporting the Confederacy during the War and saying bad things about Mr. Lincoln. I guess *they* know better than those who lived at that time too! It must be a very fine thing to have a God's eye view of human history.

*

Not to be outdone in the sesquicentennial celebration, the Public Broadcast System (PBS) trotted out their fundraising arse in the hole—I mean ace in the hole—Ken Burns of PBS's 'The Civil War' fame, for a new 'documentary' called 'The Address.' PBS described the production as

> ...a 90-minute feature length documentary ... [that] tells the story of a tiny [government indoctrination camp—Just kidding—sort of... not really...] school in Putney, Vermont, the Greenwood School, where each year the students are encouraged to practice, memorise, and recite the Gettysburg Address. In its exploration of the Greenwood School, the film claims to also unlock the history, context and importance of President Lincoln's most powerful address.

To build momentum for the new documentary and get folks involved, people all over the country—all over the 'nation' in their words—were encouraged to memorise the Gettysburg Address and upload a video of them reciting it. I counted 1,342 uploaded videos on the LearntheAddress.com website sometime in 2020.[5]

---

[5]   This website is currently offline (or dead). You can find it archived here: bit.ly/pbs-learn-the-address.

You might recognise the names of a few of the participants:

Presidents Jimmy 'P-Nut' Carter, King Bush the First, Little Bush (AKA 'Shrub'), and Barry Obama (lama-ding-dong)[6]. Other participants included the always charming and lovely Nancy Pelosi of the U.S. House of Representatives (we're not exactly sure who or what she represents); the always insightful and impartial Wolf Blitzer of CNN, financial daredevil Warren Buffet; the heretofore missing-in-action queen of 70s comedy Carol Burnett; philanthropist nerd Bill 'The Vaxinator' Gates; Whoopi 'WTF' Goldberg of the always entertaining, informative, and impartial daytime drama *The View*; Jimmy 'I always look stoned' Kimmel of *Late Night* fame; Newswoman (we think) and political commentator Rachel Maddow; the New England financial guru and home décor diva, Martha Stewart; and America's favourite Irish-Americans, Conan O'Brien and Bill O'Reilly.

To see aforementioned video (and you really should), use the QR code above or this URL: bit.ly/TheAddress-2013.

With this cast of illustrious characters endorsing the project— many, many equally illustrious names having been omitted (to save space and cut back on the number of insults so that I might spend less time in purgatory)—you might ask:

'Who are you, you uneducated, knuckle-dragging, Southern nobody, to analyse or criticise Lincoln's most 'inspirational' address when so many luminaries, including (*may God have mercy upon us!*) experts, politicians, reporters, newscasters, performing artists, and giants of industry and finance clearly reverence the address and believe in the veracity of its contents?'

---

6    There is a song that comes to mind whenever I hear that name: bit.ly/shama-lama. I don't know why.

Well, my dear reader, you got me there! I am nobody much, as far as most everyone is concerned, compared to those public servants and defenders of 'our democracy,' (whatever *that* is) but I do like consistency, something that doesn't seem to bother *those people* as long as it gets them closer to where they want to go (and take us kicking and screaming along with them).

I will be the first to freely admit that the *words* of the Gettysburg Address are pretty, indeed, lofty, stirring, enchanting—even mesmerising—but such considerations only address questions of FORM and not SUBSTANCE.

*The question that was never raised*—during the sesquicentennial anniversary of Lincoln's speech, its aftermath, or in other articles and publications that have come down and continue to come down to us to the present day—*is whether or not the seductive words of this cunning linguist and master debater, Abraham Lincoln, were TRUE.*

# I.

# OUR FATHERS DID NO SUCH THING

'Four score and seven years ago our fathers brought forth on this continent, a *new nation...*' (emphasis added)

**AS MUCH AS LINCOLN** may have wished it to be the case, no *new nation* was brought forth on the American continent 'four score and seven years' before his speech.

In 1776, thirteen English colonies, with thirteen different governing bodies (out of 20 English colonies on the continent and in the Caribbean),[7] collectively declared the reasons why they thought it necessary to sever their ties, that is, to *secede*[8] from their mother country.

---

7 Namely, Newfoundland, Nova Scotia, Bermuda, Bahamas, Jamacia, British Leeward Island, and Barbados. Farther south was British Honduras. Even though it is more precise to say, 'the 13 English Colonies,' and follow this by enumerating each colony by name, I will use (for my own sanity and perhaps yours as well, dear reader) the more familiar appellation of 'the Colonies' or the 'American Colonies' or even the 'British American Colonies' unless a specific point needs to be made. (Let's hope that doesn't happen!) It is an important detail, in my humble opinion. The rest stayed as they were for the time... Our neighbours to the north, Canada, maintain (although very loosely now) their ties with the Mother Country

8 Lincoln's position on secession was summed up in the following: 'Plainly the central idea of secession is the essence of anarchy...' First Inaugural Address, March 4, 1861. *Is it?* We'll look at the First Inaugural a little later, but not his bit on 'anarchy.'

They were 'held together' by common practical interest, nothing more. It was mutually beneficial to unite for the purposes of defence against an aggressor that meant to subjugate and deny them the rights, privileges, and representation in their own assemblies of governance to which they had come to enjoy over the course of many, many years. The colonists were not inventing something new; they were protecting something old, namely, self-government and their inherited rights as Englishmen which was being threatened by the English Parliament and allowed by the only sovereign they recognised, namely, King George III. Anyone who says that America was founded on anything other than this, an idea[9] or 'proposition,' for example, has missed the entire essence of the War for American Independence.[10]

## THE CONTINENTAL CONGRESSES

Separation was not the colonists' first choice, it was reconciliation. Prior to 1776 the colonists sent remonstrances to the King and made every effort to bring to heel, in the words of Thomas Jefferson, the

> ...unwarrantable encroaches and usurpations, attempted to be made by the legislature of one part of the empire, upon those rights which God and the laws have given equally and independently to all....'[11]

---

You cannot hold this position and also hold the position of save the "nation" that came out of the act of secession—that is, when British American Colonies declared their independence *from* the country of King George III . Maybe it's only "anarchy" only if a certain someone is in charge, *eh?*

9   I've had many people tell me that America is an *idea*. I guess that means that wherever you happen to live *in* America it does not make you an American as such, but rather, it *is* an idea—it resides in the mind. Thus, it is conceivable that a 'right-thinking' person on the other side of the world is an American and may be even more American than you unless you share the same idea. This 'America-as-an-idea' business comes with a cost. Ideas not based on real things (like your home or your family) will do that. It has done that. We pay for it every day.

10   I purposefully avoid 'American Revolution' because the colonists were trying to preserve their rights, not create new ones.

11   Thomas Jefferson, 'A Summary View of the Rights of British America' (1774). Quick Link: bit.ly/1774-summary-view (Accessed 05 December 2022).

In other words, for the King to interpose on the behalf of the British American subjects, against the unprecedented machinations of the British Parliament (in which they had no representation). Jefferson's tone, while firm, still held out the hope of reconciliation, not division:

> This, sire, is our last, our determined resolution; and that you will be pleased to interpose with that efficacy which your earnest endeavours may insure to procure redress of these great grievances, to quiet the minds of your subjects in British America, against any apprehensions of future encroachment, to establish fraternal love and harmony throughout the whole empire, and that these may continue to the latest ages of time, is the fervent prayer of all British America![12]

This was not the first time British America appealed to their king. It had been an ongoing affair, beginning (as far as I can tell) with a series of remonstrances and resolutions by individual colonies in the 1760s in response to the Sugar, Currency, and Stamp Acts,[13] that eventually led to the First Continental Congress (1774), a representative body of the various colonies that gathered to determine what course of action they should take to collectively respond to these acts of usurpation by Parliament which had become intolerable to them.

Why?

Since the first English settlement at Jamestown in 1607 (no, my dear friends, it was not Plymouth, Massachusetts—that occurred in 1620), and in each successive settlement, the colonists

---

12  *Ibid.*

13  For example, New York's petition of October 18, 1754, Massachusetts' Protest of November 3, 1764, Virginia's petition of December 18, 1864, Pennsylvania's Resolves of September 21, 1765, the Connecticut Resolves of October 25, 1765, and South Carolina's Resolves of November 29, 1765, to name a few. See Shain, Barry Allen, *The Declaration of Independence in Historical Context: American State Papers, Petitions, Proclamations, & Letters of the Delegates to the First National Congresses* (Indianapolis: Liberty Find, 2014), pp. 35-88.

had enjoyed, *by royal charter*, the same privileges and inherited rights they would have enjoyed if they had remained in the mother country:

> All persons, being English subjects and inhabiting the colonies, and every of their children born therein, were declared to have and possess all liberties, franchises, and immunities, within any other dominion of the crown, to all intents and purposes, as if they had been abiding and born within the realm of England, or any other dominion of the crown.[14]

The first Continental Congress adopted what was then called the *Continental Association* or *Articles of Association* to collectively deal with the issues they faced. This association could hardly be said to be the preamble to the creation of a nation, although Lincoln certainly thought so, as evidenced in his first inaugural address. While it is outside of the scope of this work to enumerate their grievances and responses taken up by the First Continental Congress, it is interesting to note that their adoption of the 'non-importation, non-consumption, non-exportation' of British goods—what we would call a boycott—opened with a pledge of loyalty to the King.

I'm not trying to belabour the point (or am I?), but this was a mere association of loyal subjects, each representing the interest of their own communities, attempting to persuade the King to secure their collective rights which each colony had enjoyed under their separate and distinct Royal Colonial Charters and the English Constitution. They figured collective bargaining had a better chance of success and went with it. There is nothing revolutionary about this. The King wasn't following the laws and they wanted to persuade him to do so.

---

14    Jonathan Elliot, 'Sketch of Ante-Revolutionary History,' *The Debates in the Several State Conventions on the Adoption of the Federal Constitution* (1830, Altenmünster, Germany: Jazzybee Verlag, 2018), Vol. I, p. 20.

By the time the Congress of Colonies (AKA, the Second Continental Congress) met again in May of 1775, the cold war of words had become a hot war of men and arms—the Battles of Lexington and Concord—along with other violent altercations of various sizes—having already soiled the ground with blood. Still, even when independence seemed, and indeed turned out to be, the only way forward, the Congress *still* sought a peaceful resolution to the strife as evidenced by the *Olive Branch Petition* of July 8, 1775.[15]

These are not the acts of men trying to establish a 'new nation.' Even *The unanimous Declaration of the thirteen united States of America*[16]—what is now referred to as simply 'The Declaration of Independence' (for some reason)—does not hint at any desire or intention to create a new nation, only—given the ongoing outrages by King and Parliament, which were enumerated in detail in the document itself—that 'these United Colonies [plural] are, and of Right, ought to be Free and Independent States [plural],' together with all the powers associated therewith. By declaring themselves to be *States* they were not saying they were like Mississippi, Vermont, or North Carolina in the way that we have come to 'use' the word 'State,' but more like, France, Germany, and even Great Britian.[17]

[Let that sink in for a moment... It's important to understand how *they* saw *themselves*.]

As we all know, this collective bargaining did not work. In fact, things got worse as time progressed.

*

---

15   Shain, The Declaration of Independence in Historical Context, pp. 290-293.

16   Hereafter, any shortening of the full title of the document is for the sake of convenience only—it would be tedious on both the reader and the writer to write that long (albeit important) title over and over.

17   This is evidenced by the Treatise of Paris (see Appendix B) by naming each colony and gaining their independence by name.

Can the United States be one thing—a nation born in 1776—if the document to which Lincoln refers in his Address as *the* document that marks the birth of his imaginary nation says in its very title that there are *Thirteen united States of America*?

This question, of course, is rhetorical.

The meaning and implication should be plain to any honest mind even slightly familiar with this time period and the documents and actions (either by individual colonies, or collectively in the colonial/ continental congresses) which preceded this joint declaration to the world which explains and justifies their act of secession from their mother country.

I make no claim here to have given a comprehensive account of the events leading to the joint Declaration of Independence of July 4, 1776, to which Lincoln points to as the birth of his imaginary nation, only enough to show that there was no intention of creating a nation, nor did there exist any American Nation in 1776.

## THE FIRST AMERICAN CONSTITUTION

As I have already shown, there was no formal agreement binding those 13 colonies together in 1776. It may be characterised—at best—as a loosely constructed alliance between interested parties. It was *The Articles of Confederation and perpetual Union between the States of New Hampshire, Massachusetts-bay, Rhode Island and Providence Plantations, Connecticut, New York, New Jersey, Pennsylvania, Delaware, Maryland, Virginia, North Carolina, South Carolina, and Georgia* of 1777—the first American Constitution—which *did* formalise the nature of their association— but would not be ratified by *all* of the participating colonies, now independent States, until 1781. But since that document expressly declared that each State retained (*not* gained) its 'sovereignty, freedom, and independence,'[18] one would be hard-pressed to call this voluntary union of States a 'nation.'

---

18   See Treaty of Paris, Appendix A.

Just as there was no nation in 1776, there was no nation created by the First American Constitution, AKA, The Articles of Confederation, when fully ratified by the several States in 1781.

Sadly, the Articles of Confederation—the document birthed in the American War for Independence—is all but lost to American consciousness. If one were only exposed to a college level survey of American History, they would come away believing that there was a Declaration of Independence, followed by a 'revolutionary' war, and concluded by the quick adoption and ratification of what is commonly referred to as *the* U.S. Constitution.

The Articles, if mentioned at all, are usually portrayed as a weak and unworkable document that brighter minds had the good sense to toss on the garbage heap to create a 'more perfect union.'

But was it?

The Articles of Confederation was *the* Constitution of the 13 United States. It was the terms on which and with which the former colonies would associate and cooperate with one another as a collection or union of States (think countries) and to which every State, in their sovereign capacity freely ratified.[19] The word 'united' is lower case throughout the Articles because it was a descriptive term, not a title as such, except in Article I.

This was a fact that no one at the time disputed—a fact that was still understood by most Americans, even after the adoption of the Second Constitution of 1787.

This was not a myth dreamed up by States' Rights 'schemers' like John C. Calhoun to protect 'the slave power' as many of us were taught and a majority of us—with scant exception—have come to believe. It was a well-known, commonly accepted, and well documented fact:

---

19   It was kind of like the European Union which, to my knowledge, has never declared itself to be a nation, or denied a member State to choose freely to withdraw ('secede,' in good ole rebel parlance) from the union (BREXIT, for example)—at least not yet! I had a hard time wrapping my mind around this until I read the Treaty of Paris and the Articles of Confederation to understand how they saw themselves, and how they saw each other. Both are in the Appendix (A & B).

the States made the union; the union was a creature of the States, and as such, the union was not sovereign in and of itself. It was established for specific and enumerated purposes on behalf of the States and only those purposes. That's it!

The Articles provided 1 vote to every State, and it took a unanimous vote to amend it, not a mere majority or super majority, *it took ALL OF THEM* as co-equal members of a community of sovereign States—what they called a 'league of friendship' which was to be perpetual.[20]

States Rights were not, in the parlance of our betters, some form of neo-Confederate revisionism, they were (and still are) the foundation, indeed the bedrock, on which the Union—in whatever form it took, whether under the First American Constitution or the Second American Constitution—squarely and solidly rests.

There is no 'compact theory,' that stands in contradistinction to the 'nationalist theory,' both of which may be said to be equally plausible. The nature of both governing documents *were as compacts* between sovereign societies (referred to as States).[21] Anyone who defends the 'nationalist theory' has to go around their ass to get to their elbow to spin it in any other way.

This false rendering of plain history and documented facts could only be rendered 'true' (politically true, or 'politically correct') by bullets, bombs, and bayonets, that is, total war as well as by the skillful silencing of dissenting voices wherever they could be reached so that only one version of American history—the nationalist version—would be left.

This was done by Lincoln and the Republican Party with the hope, one assumes, that what *really* happened could be driven from the collective memory after a sufficient amount of time and conditioning. Can I prove that this was Lincoln's actual intention?

---

20  The notion of 'perpetual union' will be addressed in a later chapter.

21  Dr. Brion McClanahan has called it the 'Compact Fact' and rightly so.

No. But I can make the argument that he was less than honest (*i.e.*, a liar) and knew that his telling of the birth of the American nation had nothing to do with reality.

Perhaps he thought the Union of 1787 *should have been* a national and not a federal style of government, but that was not the kind of government with which he was participating as president—poorly, I might add.

The consequence of all this, in our own time, is the inability of otherwise normal and rational thinking people to see what is right in front of them—that there was no nation and that there is no nation—at least not one legally established and freely chosen by the people of the several States as had been done under *both* Constitutions.[22]

## THE SECOND AMERICAN CONSTITUTION

*The Constitution for the United States*—better described as the Second American Constitution for our purposes—which terminated the constitutional compact created by the *Articles of Confederation*—would not go into effect until the summer of 1788 (a dozen years from 1776), when 11[23] of the 13 States ratified it and made the document binding, but *only on those States so ratifying.*[24]

If this created a nation—one and indivisible—as we are told *ad nauseum* through post-bellum nationalist history books, the so-

---

22　Note the new constitution required 9 states, not 51% of the American People in the aggregate—something no one would have even contemplated at the time—everyone knew who the principals were (States) and who the agent was. Principals always hold the reins of power, although they can freely delegate certain functions, as indeed they did and would do during the adoption of the Second American Constitution.

23　The document states that it needed only 9 to start the new union, which might have had 9 to 13 (or even more) members States, although that was not a foregone conclusion. They were being presented a document they did not ask for, was not even similar to what they had been sent and authorized to do, and would create a Union government structure with MORE POWER, including the ability to TAX. (What were they thinking?!?!)

24　They didn't pull the proverbial trigger until they got New York and Virginia signed-up, so they waited on them; hence, eleven before it was formally established.

called pledge of allegiance,[25] and other means of perpetuating the 'Proposition Nation' myth, the sovereign States that pre-existed this new political arrangement *were ignorant of this crucial detail and would not have ratified it if they thought that it did.*

The creation of these documents is a curious one and the differences between the two American constitutions are striking (See Appendix C).

The gathering was billed as a convention to remedy the alleged defects of the Articles of Confederation, indeed, the credentials of each delegate representing their particular State *only provided the authority to propose amendments to the existing constitution*, NOT to create a new one.

Here are a few examples, including some smaller fragments so as to establish this was not an isolated position, but one universally held amongst and between the States of the Federated Union:[26]

> ... Resolved, that the Hon. Robert Yates, John Lessing, John Lansing, Jun., and Alexander Hamilton, Esqrs., be, and they are hereby, declared duly nominated and appointed delegates, on the part of this state, to meet such delegates as may be appointed on the part of the other states, respectively, on the second Monday in May next, at Philadelphia, *for the sole and expressed purpose of revising the Articles of Confederation ...* *[to] render the Federal Constitution adequate to the*

---

25  Author of the 'Pledge,' defrocked minister and socialist, Francis Bellamy, once said that it [the pledge] 'encompassed our struggle for independence and for indivisibility, which the Civil War was required to fully prove.' You see, indivisibility, dear reader, is not determined by law, custom, presidents, or anything else, it is *proved* by armed conflict. I should not have to tell you that this is complete bovine manure. 2 + 2 = 4 does not depend on whether or not I can kick the math teacher's ass, does it? Does any truth rest on who can kill more than the other? If it does, I have very different understandings on the nature of 'truth.' Plato, through the voice of Socrates, takes up the question of 'might makes right' in the first chapter of *The Republic*. It's worth reading.

26  See Elliot, 'Credentials of Members of the Federal Convention,' *Debated in the Several State Conventions on the Adoption of the Federal Constitution* (1830), Vol. I, pp. 105ff.

*exigencies of government and the preservation of the Union...* (Emphasis added)

—State of New York

... Be it therefore by the Commonwealth of Virginia, that seven commissioners be appointed... to join with them [Delegates from the participating States] in devising and discussing all such alterations and further provisions as may be necessary *to render the Federal Constitution* [The Articles] *adequate to the exigencies of the Union...*[27]

—Commonwealth of Virginia (Emphasis added)

... [A]re hereby appointed from this state to meet in the Convention of the deputies of other states... and join with them in *devising,* deliberating on, and discussing, such alterations and further provisions as may be necessary *to render the Federal Constitution* [The Articles] *adequate to the exigencies of the Union* ... provided that such alterations or further provisions, or any of them, do not extend to the part of the 5th article of the Confederation of the said states...[28]

—Delaware State (Emphasis added)

... [T]o join with such deputies (they being duly authorized and empowered) in devising, all such alterations, clauses, articles, and provisions, as may be thought necessary *to render the Federal Constitution* [The Articles] *entirely adequate to the*

---

27  John Blair, James Madison, George Mason, James McClurg, Edmund Randolph, George Washington, and George Wythe. The Commonwealth wanted Patrick Henry to be a delegate and his name is on the original list, but Mr. Henry declined, purported saying that he 'smelled a rat.'

28  Article 5 states that 'In determining questions in the United States in Congress Assembled, each state shall have 1 vote.' See Articles of Confederation, Appendix B.

*actual situation and future good government of the confederated states ...*

—State of South Carolina (Emphasis added)

... [F]or the purpose of revising the Federal Constitution [Again (Sigh!), The Articles] ... to render the Federal Constitution adequate to the exigencies of the Union ...

—State of Maryland (Emphasis added)

... [F]or the purpose of *revising the Federal Constitution...* [No need to say it again. I'm sure it's aggravating!] (Emphasis added)

—The State of North Carolina

The fact that The Articles of Confederation WAS THE FEDERAL CONSTITUTION (and was referred to as such) when *some* of the delegates trotted off to Philadelphia to do away with it.

This fact may just be an important detail in the understanding of how things actually happened.

I have not had one person so far accurately answer the following question: How many constitutions has the United States had since the American War for Independence?

'One,' is the only answer I have gotten so far—and not from people off the streets, but many well-informed people of my acquaintance!

Up until my research for this book, I would have answered the same!

*Surprise! There are two!*

This should be common knowledge, but it is not.

*Why isn't it?*

Why didn't I know that there was a constitution preceding the only constitution I ever knew to exist?

*Why are the Articles referred to as an 'agreement,' 'governing document,' or some equally descriptive term that obfuscates The Articles' true character in the relevant literature?*

The people and their representative bodies called the Articles the 'Federal Constitution,' or 'Federated Constitution'—why not use that?

Has no one in academia—or elsewhere—picked-up a primary source document or is something else at play?

It's unbelievable, I know, but we really need to get back on track.

Sorry for the rant.

Let's continue, shall we?

*

Almost as soon as the doors were shut, the curtains drawn, and a pact of secrecy was made between the participants, the Articles were 'determined' to be beyond repair and a *new* constitution would be constructed and presented to the States. New constitutions such as the Virginia Plan—an outline for a NATIONAL GOVERNMENT— were put forth *immediately* and with *aforethought*, having been prepared by Madison. This 'founding father' also had the Virginia delegation arrive days earlier to jockey for position. The Virginians even brought General George Washington to preside for good measure![29] (I mean, who would or could—given his legendary status and sterling reputation—oppose anything in which General Washington was involved, right?)

---

29  There is no way for me to know this one way or the other, but after what I've encountered as I researched the items in this little book—I'll be honest—I have begun to wonder about a lot of things regarding that thing on the banks of the Potomac River we call 'the government'... Just being honest.

These actions can only be interpreted, in my simple way of thinking, that they never intended to amend (or attempt to amend) the Federal Constitution or Articles—the only thing they had the authority to do.

While this *might* not rise to the charge of treason against the States these men represented (or does it?), it comes about as close to treason as you can get without finding yourself taking a long walk on a short rope, if you know what I mean (treason being a hangin' offence in those days...).

## TROUBLING IMPLICATIONS

I have to stop and wonder at the larger issues here—things that don't jive with what I thought I knew (i.e., what I was taught and believed to be true until I was well into my 30s). This is difficult for me to do, dear readers, given the reverence given by many, if not most hard-working, God fearing, decent Americans to these 'framers' of 'THE' constitution and the document itself—BUT these 'framers,' or a not insignificant number of them, colluded, with aforethought, to overthrow the existing political order, that is, to overthrow the Federal Constitution of 1781, and thus the 'freedom, sovereignty, and independence' of the States they could convince to adopt the document of this bloodless *coup d'état.* (I know, it really sounds 'blasphemous' when you put it that way, but an examination of the documents now available leaves little room for doubt, at least for me...).

Here's the rub: These supposed patriotic men did not only fail to amend the Federal Constitution as they were authorised to do, but they never even tried—indeed, never intended to try! Instead, they came shufflin' to Philly with pre-written outlines of new constitutions they hoped to push through on their *own* initiative and *own* volition—the Virginia plan, for example—even though:

1.  No one asked them to do so (in fact the opposite being the case, as we have seen above)

2.  They did so with aforethought, purposefully disregarding the instructions of their very own government—their Country, that is, their State...

In other words, they just decided that they knew better. Who does this kind of thing? Imagine something like this happening today—and it certainly could be done. Even if their *intentions* were good and their *hearts* were in the right place. Even if they thought they were 'saving the Union or some other 'righteous' cause, this ain't right.

Their *actions* were in direct *violation* of their *commissions*. In saying this, do not let it be understood that I am somehow against the Constitution of 1787 as ratified. I think it *could* have made a very fine country if it had not been continuously violated by 'the government' created by the instrument (it's not even reformable—almost nothing it does is *legal*, which is just another way of saying *Constitutional*).[30]

I'm not trying to belabour the point (or am I?), but the whole affair does not pass the sniff test, in fact, it stinks! One of America's most beloved patriots thought the very same thing—and he was chosen by Virginia to be a delegate to the Philadelphia convention. Patrick 'Give me Liberty or give me Death' Henry, was reported to have said that he 'smelled a rat' and *refused* to attend. [31]

It would be DECADES before any journal of an attending member was published, or the details of the States' ratifying conventions were collected and made available in a multi-volume collection. But by then, the damage was done and almost beyond repair. This occurred in large part by the actions of the 'supreme' court and Joseph Story's three volume nationalist interpretation of America's Founding, its constitution, and its laws—*Commentaries on the constitution of the United States: with a preliminary review*

---

30  As I understand it (and the way it was clearly understood during the early days of the Federation of States), the Constitution *as ratified* is the measuring stick by which we determine what is federal law and what is not (or by definition, cannot be).

31  There were others who did not attend for various reasons or left when they saw what it was. In fact, Rhode Island sent no one! They probably smelled a rat too!

*of the constitutional history of the colonies and states before the adoption of the constitution (1833).*[32] (But that is a *story* for another day, get it?).

Who knew, before the journals of Robert Yates or James Madison, were published (decades after the ratification of the Second American Constitution) that supposed luminaries such as Alexander Hamilton—whose machinations in post-ratification America were cut short by Aaron Burr in a duel[33]—took a monarchical view of what the form of government should be under the 'new constitution.' Among other things, he wanted an executive who would serve a lifetime tenure, for States to be mere 'election districts' of this government, governors of each State to be appointed by the executive, veto power over State laws, along with other abominations you are free to look up. Knowing now, what they did not know then, Hamilton's essays in the *Federalist* seem (and I'd say are) wiggly and disingenuous. Same for Madison, in my humble and unsophisticated reading of the available material, although to a lesser degree.

---

32   In the preface of this tome, Story says, 'From two great sources, however, I have drawn by far the greatest part of my most valuable materials. These are, The Federalist, an incomparable commentary of three of the greatest statesmen of their age, and the extraordinary Judgments of Mr. Chief Justice Marshall upon constitutional law.' Not the greatest sources to convey how things really happened and what they meant. Lawyers are usually exposed to this work during Law School. It seems to ruin a large number of them.

Note that Story did *not* consult the journals of the participants or the State ratification documents. Most of them were still unpublished at that time... (Oh, what luck!)

33   A good thing, although unfortunate for him in my estimation, as he had already caused more mischief than any other public figure (outside of the courts, who consisted of a gaggle of Centralisers/Nationalist/Monarchist geese like himself) in his own day. His influence continues to burden the people of the several States right down to this very day (and I am excluding the horror of that ridiculous musical 'Hamilton' which is an abomination in its portrayal of the scheming bastard (literally) as a hero, not the behind-the-scenes mischief making weasel that he really was).

Don't take my word for it. Check out *Hamilton's Curse* by Dr.Thomas DiLorenzo and *How Alexander Hamilton Screwed up America* by Dr. Brion McClanahan for all the dirty details.

Be sure to check out the citations for yourself. They are both on solid ground, in my humble opinion. Plus, you need to see for yourself. We cannot always rely on the 'experts,' who are human, fallible, and better not get out of line or they'll lose their jobs! We all have interests. Some interests, I venture to say, are more honourable than others.

Why else promote the government neither really wanted and Hamilton completely despised?[34]

\*

As an aside, I would be suspicious if, in our own time, instead of offering amendments to the current constitution to remedy a certain 'problem,' our 'leaders' (after a closed door and secretive meeting) determined 'we' would be better off with an entirely new constitution that gives 'them' a few more enumerated powers.

I assume most of you would be suspicious as well, knowing human beings to be what they are and politicians, a sub-species of human beings (as history and recent memory seem to suggest) are likely to do if you 'give them an inch' even if they promise—in writing, no less—not to 'take a yard.'

If such a thing were accomplished, as it was in 1787-1788, that *inch given* would become a yard, then a mile, until it eventually (in our own day) would become a world-wide empire with a standing army and hundreds of military installations in 80 countries across the world.[35]

Do you think 'we,' in this 'enlightened age,' would quickly adopt a new constitution? I would not be comfortable with that, especially if 'our' current crop of leaders were involved with it in any way, shape, or form.

Yet this is exactly what was being asked of the States when they were presented with the Second American Constitution.

How'd that work out for us?

\*

---

34  Of Hamilton, Madison said, 'No man's ideas were more remote from the plan [proposed constitution] than his own ...' *The Papers of James Madison*, ed. Henry Gilpin (Washington: Langtree & O'Sullivan, 1840), Vol. III, p. 1601.

35  Doug Bandow, '750 Bases in 80 Countries Is Too Many for Any Nation: Time for the US to Bring Its Troops Home,' Cato Institute (cato.org), (Accessed 10 November 2023). See bit.ly/750bases.

The whole gathering at Philadelphia in 1787 was b.s. from the get-go, and even though the States did eventually pass the proposed constitution, making it the law of the land, it did *not* create a national government, although the so-called Federalists (who were actually somewhere on the spectrum between centralisers and monarchists, something no one outside of this 'secret circle' knew at the time of ratification) did their best to create a national or strongly centralised government in Philadelphia.

Of course, after the ratification of the requisite number of States, many of these 'founding fathers,' particularly those who called themselves *Federalists*, went to work loading-up the federal court with those of their ilk, invading States without their consent (Whisky Rebellion), chartering a bank (which was rejected at the convention and is, therefore, not among the delegated powers presented to the States), and during the Adams administration, the Alien and Sedition Act, which forbade criticism of the government (a clear violation of the first amendment) just to name a few—ALL illegal under *their own description* of what the document did and did not do (but that is a story for another day).

I find it interesting, especially with regards to Lincoln's false rendering of history at Gettysburg, that neither the word 'perpetual' nor 'nation,' nor 'national,' nor any other phrase that suggests that America was anything other than a confederation or union of sovereign States, appear in the constitution Lincoln swore as president to defend, although there was *nothing to prevent the 'framers' from using this characterisation or carrying over the perpetuity clause.* (This will be more fully examined in another chapter.)

## MOVING ON

The new constitution was hotly debated in many States and a few passed it by rather thin margins—some only with the assurance that a 'Bill of Rights' would be added to the document upon the first gathering of the new government.

Why?

Were they afraid that their States would infringe on their personal 'rights'?

Uh, hell no!

They already had these rights, and these rights were protected by tradition and their own constitutions.

Rather, knowing that to 'give an inch' is to risk 'losing a yard' (or more),[36] they wanted to *bind* the new government down and forbid them from meddling in the fundamental rights they fought to preserve in their war for independence.

The keystone of the Bill of Rights—the one that made all the other amendments and the constitution itself a document that provided only for enumerated and expressly delegated powers was the 10th amendment which explicitly and unequivocally states that

> The powers not *delegated* to the United States by the Constitution, nor *prohibited* by it to the States, are *reserved to the States respectively, or to the people.*

Next time someone says that they have some constitutional right or other, tell them that the Constitution of 1787, as ratified, HAD NO AMENDMENTS or BILL OF RIGHTS. There is no such a thing as a First Amendment Right to Free Speech, for example. The first amendment was added to keep CONGRESS away from censorship or other means of suppressing language (and certainly not to enforce it or define it). If you read through the Articles and other documents mentioned herein, you will be better able to understand who these people were and what they did (or did not) agree to. If you have a right, dear reader, it didn't come from an amendment to that constitution.

---

36  I don't know if this is a uniquely Southern witticism, but my Momma used it: 'I give you kids an inch and you take a yard!'

I know this is shocking, given the way we talk of various kinds of rights said to derive their legitimacy because a constitution was amended. (*God, help us!*)

Those opposed to the ratification of this new constitution were largely responsible for insuring the adoption and passage of the Bill of Rights. These patriots were called 'Anti-Federalist' by the Federalists (although *they* were, in fact, the *real* federalists and called themselves 'republicans').

These amendments were added as an *assurance* that the Federal Government would have *nothing whatsoever to say* about the establishment of religion, exercise of free speech, freedom of the press, the right to bear arms, etc. It was taken, explicitly taken, *entirely from their jurisdiction.* Every single last one of them. That was the whole point of putting them there!

Those were, and legally remain, in the hands of the States and the States alone regardless of what the Oracles on the 'Supreme' court in the District of Criminals (DC) might happen to divine from their reading of the tea leaves or the Ouija board they keep on hand for interpreting 'Constitutional Law' (which everyone knows is rooted in case law, partisan politics, and a lot of b.s. they just made-up on the fly, depending on who was in power and which way the wind was blowing).

Like most of American history and jurisprudence, things are the mirror opposite of what they appear and purport to be.

*Plus ça change, plus c'est la même chose.*[37]

Regardless, it can be said without equivocation and with ample documentary evidence—from the journals of the participants of the 'Constitutional Convention' in 1787, to the printed defences *of* or opposition *to* the document, to the actual ratification debates in the several States—that the States acceded to a Federal and *not* a

---

37  The more things change, the more things stay the same (attributed to Jean-Baptiste Alphonse Karr).

national model of government.[38] Even James Madison, the 'father' of THE constitution, makes this clear in the popular, but in most cases irrelevant[39] collection of essays called *The Federalist*.

Maybe that's not what some of the 'framers' *wanted*, but that's what the people *approved* through their representatives in the State conventions—the only place legitimacy resides in a federated republic of republics.[40]

Of course, none of the States were obliged to ratify the new constitution and could have rejected it had they wanted to, but as it turned out—for better or for worse—they did, although some States took longer to do so than others.

They were most certainly *not* part of a nation dedicated to a proposition created in 1776 (or any other date) and from which there was no escape—never ever—regardless of the reason.

Who would sign up, dear reader, for such a horror without a gun in their mouth or bayonet at their breast?

Even a Marital union—which is perpetual by its very nature (i.e., a lifetime commitment based on a series of vows or promises)—ceases to be perpetual in the case of abuse, abandonment, or infidelity.[41]

---

38   If anyone can show me around this problem that does not employ 'Universal Law,' then I'd love to hear it. Just go to ShotwellPublishing.com and mash ('click') the menu item 'Contact us.' I would really be interested.

39   It doesn't matter what Hamilton and Madison thought of the Constitution of 1787, although they might provide some insight in some instances. What matters is what the States understood the document meant.

*The Federalist* is insightful as two of the authors (namely, Madison and Hamilton— John Jay was abroad at the time) were actually involved in the drafting process and would have first-hand knowledge of what was said and how it was understood at the convention (secret cabal?), but once again, as good as some of the essays may be, the architects of the new constitution were not a party to the compact, only the States 'so ratifying' were.

40   See Article IV, section 4, of the Second American Constitution.

41   The so-called 'no-fault' divorce notwithstanding. Either the vows made between the betrothed are binding, or the institution (even as defined for us today by a court that calls itself supreme somewhere up there 'north of Richmond') is a farce. What else can you call it?

What some folks are now calling—a 'national divorce'—was certainly appropriate (and legal) in the 1860s and may even be more desirable and justifiable today.

The *USS Titanic* is sinking, and no one has even considered the 50 lifeboats currently available—but in poor shape after decades and decades of neglect and abuse—to break free. I can think of no reason to go down with the ship if there is an alternative way forward.

## CONCLUSION

Given the foregoing, we are led to the obvious and irrefutable conclusion (and this is the point of all that mess above) that since there was no nation in 1776, 1781 or 1788, there was no 'nation' when Lincoln's speech was delivered in 1863 (or today, for that matter, at least not legally).

There certainly *had been* a voluntary union of States created by the *Second American Constitution*, but by 1861 this political arrangement—like the union created by the *Articles of Confederation* (which explicitly states that it was 'perpetual')[42]—*had been terminated* by the solemn conventions of no less than eleven sovereign States in the South—some of these conventions were illegally broken-up by the 'national authority.'

The only thing that had occurred 'four score and seven years' before Lincoln's address was that thirteen independent political societies formally and publicly declared their reasons for seceding from a government that they viewed as hostile to their inherited way of life and traditionally recognised rights.

Nothing more.

The story told by Lincoln regarding 'the birth of a nation' was false then and it is false now.

I know some of you are trying to find a way around this, but ask yourself why you are compelled to do so.

---

42   See the text of The Articles of Confederation in Appendix 'B.'

Just take a deep breath and let's do some more exploring... There's nothing to lose other than a false understanding of historical events which can only make things worse (as more falsehoods are piled on this particular falsehood).

Sorry! One more thing:

## WHAT ABOUT THE NEW STATES?

In case you are tempted to say that *maybe* the 13 original States that *ratified* the Constitution, thereby creating a new federal government, *might* have a case for pursuing a form of government outside the old Union, but the newer States (14-50), as a creation of Congress, certainly do/did not... Let me stop you there!

Congress did not and does not now have the authority to *create* a State; they can only *admit* an existing State into the Union.

States are created by the sovereign act of the people in a given territory by the adoption of a constitution. Once they apply for and receive admittance into the American Union, the State or States so applying are on 'an equal footing with all the original States in every respect whatsoever...'[43]

Every reserved right belonging to the original thirteen States in ratification of the Second American Constitution is theirs as well—no exceptions given.

If they are on an equal footing with all the original States and if any of those States reserved the right to leave the union in their ratification document upon adopting the Second American Constitution (such as was *explicitly* done by Virginia, New York, and Rhode Island), they have, by implication, that same reserved right.

---

43  Extracted from a speech on the admittance of the State of Michigan into the Union by John C. Calhoun, 05 January 1837. *The Essential Calhoun: Selection from Writings, Speeches, and Letters*, ed. Clyde N. Wilson (New Brunswick & London: Transaction Publishers, 1992), p. 83.

Senator John C. Calhoun of South Carolina explains the principles at work here:

> Ours is a Federal Republic—a Union of States. Michigan is a State; a State in the course of admission, and differing only from the others States in their federal relation. She is declared to be a State in the most solemn manner by your own act. She can come into the Union only as a State; and by her voluntary assent, given by the people of the State in convention, called by the constituted authority of the State.... The relation of the citizen to the Government is through the States. They are subject to its authority and laws only because the State has assented that they should be.

The original 13, and newer States, such as Michigan, are under the authority of the general government in only certain enumerated cases, because the people of the States, through their representatives and by their own authority, *chose to be.*

In what way did this choice suggest that they gave up the right to voluntarily leave the Union if they perceived it to be a threat to their liberties and reserved rights?

They didn't.

They didn't have to.

The original 13 States (each new State being on equal footing with them) were the ones who voluntarily made the Federal Union and, thus, could reverse or rescind their membership with the very same authority. The States made the Federal Government, the Federal Government did not make the States.

The confusion about the nature of the States and their relationship to the federal government came about when unscrupulous people, like Abraham Lincoln (and others), argued that these United States had a national form of government (which is total b.s., as we have seen), although we have been forced to live in this world of falsehood where it is difficult, if not impossible in many cases, to mentally escape.

Over one hundred and fifty years of myth making has made most of us unwilling (including myself for a long time) to take a second look at this deal which does not seem to be beneficial to anyone unconnected with Washington and/or those who do its bidding.

Perhaps too much is at stake.

Perhaps we are too comfortable.

Maybe we don't want to say anything about the way we are being treated.

Maybe we are scared.

All I know is this: there was a time in this country when there was a people that said, 'ENOUGH!' and every time the usual suspects (left and right) removes or allows to be removed, a Confederate flag, plaque, monument, or some other reminder of the *true constitutionalist* who valiantly and bravely stood against the anti-constitutional usurpers in Washington, the harder it will be to set the record straight. These were the same States that created or voluntarily joined the Union whether under the First and/or Second American Constitution.

Who had the authority to tell them that they couldn't leave?

There is no such authority.

The creature cannot command the creator—even if they *think* that they can or should. Their existence depends 100% on the actions taken by the States comprising the Union.

You may disagree with the Southern States' reasons for leaving.

You may think that they would have been safer and happier in the old Union if they 'got with the programme.'

You may even think their reasons for withdrawing their membership from that union were wrong, immoral, or even repulsive, but that call is *not yours* and it *wasn't Lincoln's either.*

That determination belongs to the people of the States acting in their sovereign capacity ALONE, just as it was with the Articles of Confederation, the Constitution of 1787, and the termination of association between the Union known as the United States and most of the Southern States. Each State acting on their own volition manifested through a solemn convention of the people—the only way this kind of thing can be done.

Maybe it doesn't matter, after all these years, that we have been living a lie. I mean, what are they (the usurpers) going to do? Spy on us? Devalue the currency through spending money they don't have? Rule that a marriage is something other than what it is? Send their subjects to die in foreign lands for the business interests of our overlords and their friends around the world? Start wars without declaration? Stop a legitimate candidate running for president by tying him up in the courts? Allowing untold millions of criminal invaders to cross our borders without impunity and paying them to stay? Cheering on thugs as they burn down cities? (I could do this all day, but let this suffice for the time being.)

*Naw!* They'd never do that!

I'm pretty damn sure it matters and 'things' can never be properly addressed, much less fixed unless we face what brought us to this horror.

# II.

# Mr. Lincoln Has a Proposition For You

'...conceived in Liberty, and *dedicated to the proposition* that all men are created equal...'
(emphasis added)

**LINCOLN'S REFERENCE TO 'THE EQUALITY OF MEN'** in the *Declaration of Independence* of 1776, takes a five-word phrase out of a document of over 1300 words and imbues it with meaning which cannot be derived from either the document itself or the historical context in which it was written.

The passage from which 'the proposition' was plucked, in case it has been a while since you last read it (or heard it) goes like this...

> We hold these truths to be self-evident, that all men are created equal, that they are endowed by their Creator with certain unalienable Rights, that among these are Life, Liberty and the pursuit of Happiness... .

Many of us are so used to hearing this phrase, or parts of it, bantered around we can no longer hear what it really says. To whom was this declaration addressed? Did they mean every single person in the world, or just the parties involved?

Why employ a universal statement (ALL men) when the issue as articulated by the colonists up until independence were always rooted in specific, enumerated, complaints regarding the maintenance of their rights—not universal abstract human rights (which are imaginary)—but specific, historical rights as subjects to the British crown and heirs to the rights of Englishmen?

The first major assertion of the passage states that: 'We hold these truths to be self-evident.'

First, who is 'we'? The confederated colonists, or 'we,' all of humanity? This was not written by the finger of God, dear reader, or designed to be a template for 'America's promise,' or any other silly falsehood hoisted upon us because of our misunderstanding of both the Declaration of Independence and/or Lincoln's scandalous speech at Gettysburg. It was *WE, the States united for the cause of independence.* I don't see another reasonable conclusion to make. If you do, I'd love to hear about it. Do you? (You don't have to tell anyone!)

What does it mean that certain truths (which he later enumerates) are 'self-evident'?

Something 'self-evident,' as far as I can tell, is evidently true or accepted as such by any or all persons who LOOK[44] out and about in the world. For example, it should be self-evident to you that you are reading this sentence just as it seems self-evident to me that I am now writing it.

We can walk outside and behold the self-evident truth that it is sunny, raining, or overcast. Nothing more is needed. It is self-evidently the case.

If we are to look at an apple or an orange, it is self-evident that they are different—one is red and the other is orange, among other things. They are self-evidently not the same thing. Nothing more is needed.

---

[44]   ...or some other sense depending on the situation that is being considered.

What about the statements Jefferson employs are self-evident?

- All men are created equal; [45]

- All men are endowed by their creator with certain unalienable rights.

Are these statements *really* self-evident? I know we often *say* that they are, but are they? Were these endowments self-evident to any pre-Enlightenment era civilisation? Or at any other time in human history? Not as far as I can tell. The divine right of kings[46] was self-evident to the patriots just a few years previously. Think about it, before the war, they were singing 'God Save the King!' Washington, Madison, Hamilton, Jefferson too (and many, many more)! Why wouldn't they have? They were loyal subjects of the King. This wasn't pretend, they did not want to leave their condition as colonists and would have happily remained colonists if there hadn't been all that trouble. We do not tend to look back to the time before American independence. They were British subjects. Period.

Their inherited rights as *Englishmen*, which were being threatened by the King and Parliament, are *WHY* they declared independence in the first place. Being a subject and demanding that their rights be respected are all rolled-together in one! One does not and cannot exist without the other. (It's important to remember that George Washington was a fourth-generation British American. (Can you name your great, great grandfather?)

They were all more or less (can't speak for all the colonists) loyal subjects (more or less like we are) and did not have any inclination, until they were pushed to the wall, to do anything other than contently remain American—I mean British subjects. Some may

---

45  Setting aside the equally perplexing issue of the word 'created'—a word that is itself hierarchal: creator/created; maker/made, etc. —I do not think it necessary for our purposes of going down this theological rabbit hole, at least not in this book.

46  Which was argued against by John Locke before offering Social Contract Theory as an alternative. This, of course, provided Thomas Jefferson with much of his language we find in the preamble to the Declaration that was later used by Lincoln in his Gettysburg Address. See bonus chapter way at the end, 'SOCIAL CONTRACT THEORY AND "THE PROPOSITION."' Past the appendices. Way back there.

have seen the writing on the wall before others, but all the greatly admired 'framers' and 'Founding fathers' were to a man, BRITISH, many of them quite proud of the appellation and its heritage— especially when it came to rights they inherited as co-equal subjects of the King—as if they had been born on British soil. That is what they thought and that's why they fought.

The notion of 'unalienable rights' are certainly not self-evident for they do not appear in human history as political axioms, even within the Western tradition in a well-articulated form before the 17th century. Further, they do not appear in the arguments put forth by the colonists leading up to the Declaration, something that I hope I have established at this point.

It was not even a wide-spread position, even amongst the British and European *literati* until Thomas Hobbes, and then John Locke, worked-out detailed arguments concerning what we now call Social Contract Theory,[47] Americans in general—I think it is fair to say— were not introduced to the idea until Thomas Jefferson employed its basic tenants in the preamble to the Declaration of Independence.

While I realise that 'unalienable' is a legal term, meaning unable to take away or give up, if there is a right—by either law or custom (or both)—that appears unalienable or self-evidently to someone somewhere, that is cool with me. This is not my point. I am asking, rather, whether or not the notion of 'unalienable rights' are, in fact, self-evident. That *is* a philosophical issue. If these rights were both self-evident and unalienable, then why did this notion not grow to prominence before the so-called 'Age of Enlightenment.' To put it another way, *if* these rights were unalienable, *then* why did it take until the 1600s for anyone to fully articulate these notions.

Where did the rights enumerated by Jefferson come from?

Where do the rights enumerated in the United Nations' *Universal Declaration of Human Rights*[48] come from?

---

47  *Ibid.* I mean wayyyyyyy back there!

48  Universal Declaration of Human Rights. Adopted by the United Nations on 10 December 1948, www.un.org/en/about-us/universal-declaration-of-human-rights

To ask the question of one, is to ask the question of the other. Self-evident is a low bar—it either is or it isn't—saying 'these truths' is either 'self-evident' or 'unalienable' does not make it so. There has to be something more—a foundation (historical, philosophical, or metaphysical...) on which the claim rests. For the people of that generation, their inherited rights as Englishmen[49] or as subjects of the crown has a pedigree and could be traced back through each colonies' patrimony, which became rights as citizens of a free State.[50] These specific rights and how they were violated by King George will be enumerated below.

This is clearly new territory in British American political thought, but was the Declaration of Independence intended to be a treatise on a new political theory? I think the safer bet would be to go with what the title of the document says it is—a *declaration of the 13 united States*. This *declaration* announced to the world their (the 13 united States) intention to sever their connections to the British government and their reasoning for so doing. This was not an assemblage of words that gave magical powers to the 'government' to spread equality around the world, it was just (and I do not mean that sarcastically) a declaration of independence. Nothing more.

It did not come down from heaven, it was not written with God's finger. I'm not even sure we could say it was inspired, although the beauty and strength of the language suggest a muse of some sort. Be that as it may, their declaration put their resolution regarding their

---

(accessed 10 November 2023). Apparently these cats had access to even more self-evident and unalienable rights than Jefferson! Quick Link: bit.ly/UN-rightsX

49   This is not to say that there were no Frenchmen, Germans, or Africans in the colonies, only that the political structure, laws, culture was British. See *Albion's Seed: Four British Folkways in America* by David Hacker Fischer (Oxford University Press, 1989). There is no better work on the peculiarities British colonists brought with them and how they still have an effect on Americans (who are *always* situated in a State) up unto our very time. It's a must read, in my opinion.

50   A British serf had no notion concerning of these 'rights as Englishmen' spoken of in colonial America. These rights came about gradually, over a long period of time, through a series of negotiations, wars, or other events of give and take between the governing party(ies) and the people over which they claim authority. The Magna Carta being one of the more famous instances of rights being won by the commoners. Thus, being hard earned, they were not going to just roll over and let centuries of gradual progress be undone on their watch.

association with Great Britian out in the open. It was also giving their side of the story, getting it out there quick. They needed recognition and maybe a little foreign aid. It was both utilitarian and beautifully written, it was also a product of his fascination with the so-called 'Age of Enlightenment, particularly the work of John Locke.

The notion of *equality* expressed by Mr. Jefferson, especially given the origins of the language he employs, most assuredly has nothing to do with the modern doctrine of egalitarianism (*i.e.*, the belief in the absolute political, social, and/or economic equality of all persons as an end to be realised); *nor* is it a universal metaphysical statement pulled from the cosmic ether, *nor* is it a revealed truth by 'Nature's God.'

It's not.

It's a great document, but it's not the preamble to the creation of an indivisible nation (we can wish it otherwise, but it ain't).

It should go without saying that since there never was a nation, as described by Lincoln, it follows that there is no 'proposition,' to which it (the non-nation) could dedicate itself. *The proposition is a moot point*; NEVERTHELESS, I'd still like to take a look at the other claims made by Mr. Lincoln in this speech and hope you'll come along anyway.

It is because this nationalist error is embedded so deeply in the American psyche (including mine—you don't just free yourself of these things), I hope you will not view it to be a waste of time to enumerate the properties of a *proposition* if only to understand a *weeeeee* bit more of what is going on here. Lincoln had to have known the term and its technical meaning as an accomplished lawyer and rhetorician. How could he not?

## WHAT IS A PROPOSITION?

Briefly stated, a proposition is a statement with a truth value, that is, it can be said to be either true or false.

Not all verbal communication has this property. A question or an exclamation do not have a truth value. 'Wow!' is not true or false. 'Is it raining outside?' is not true or false; however, 'It is raining outside' can be either true or false, it depends.

Some are always true or always false by their construction alone. For example, the proposition 'It is what it is' can never be false, whereas the statement 'It is what it ain't' can never be true. The former is a tautology, the latter is a contradiction. Unlike these, the proposition 'It is raining outside' requires *something further* to determine its truth value. Looking out the window should suffice to make such a determination in this case.

So, dear reader, what are we to do to determine the truth value of the proposition 'all men are created equal'? It is not self-evidently true. It may even be self-evidently false. More information is needed.

When I look out into the world, I see people who look different, have different levels of intelligence, some are better at some things than others... We have people who are healthy and people who are sick, rich people, poor people, and people somewhere between the two; I see people with different beliefs, values, wants, desires, needs, etc. (Doesn't everyone?).

I, for example, am not very good at sports. A lot of my friends are. They are better at sports than I am. This being the case, at least with regards to our sporting abilities, we are not equal.

I think it is safe to say that we are not born equal—either in ability or circumstance—but maybe it is the 'created' bit that should be our focus, even though, admittedly, it is not something that can be pursued empirically or even by casual everyday observation, or even axiomatically from principle to principle.

This puts the proposition that 'all men are created equal' into an altogether different class of propositions—it is a statement of faith (whether the faith is religious, philosophical, or political, it makes little difference). There is no other comprehensive way of explaining this phenomenon in any other term unrelated to the notion of faith (which is not always a bad thing).

As with all statements of faith, *thousands* of interpretations attach themselves to them—perhaps self-evident according to an argument built upon certain (non-universal) faith-based premises, but in such a case, it would be self-evidently understood in different ways by different people under shifting sets of circumstances—political or otherwise.

In fact, when viewed in this light, one could justify all kinds of claims which may or may not have merit or improve the state of mankind—it would depend on who was evoking the mystical proposition and what they hoped to accomplish with it.

This line of thought is only important insofar as people *believe* that these United States are a NATION (one and indivisible) dedicated to a PROPOSITION... and there are many, probably most of whom have never even considered the consequences of such a mandate.

If a government, believing itself to be a nation dedicated to the proposition 'all men are created equal,' existed (and it does), we can expect that such a government will use its authority and all means at their disposal to *make* men equal, as *they* happen to define it, and *we* will be the guinea pigs in their various experiments trying to bring about this unnatural state of affairs.

By this I only mean that their decisions will be based on what they believe people OUGHT to be, not on how people actually ARE.

*Ought* is a tricky word and leads us to the field of ethics or moral philosophy. *Ought* requires a metaphysical foundation—take your pick, but it needs at least one. *Ought* takes us away from any proposition demonstrably true or false and depends upon a kind of political or philosophical faith (or enforcement of the tenants of the dogma). *Ought* has to be enforced if it is to be realised, especially if it is unnatural or overtly utopian. Most folks don't want you trying to improve them against their will. Especially if that 'improver' comes from a distant government and doesn't have to live the unintended consequences of their benevolent efforts.

This fact should make just about anyone who has interacted with the government at any level a little uneasy.

It is for this reason that I hold to the position that even if we were a nation (which we are not) dedicated to a proposition (which we are not), it is a bad idea for a nation, *any* nation, to dedicate themselves to a proposition, *any* proposition. Nothing good has ever come from such a thing and nothing ever will if history or human experience, born out over time and sifted out over multiple generations, is any kind of guide.

When someone (or a collection of 'someones') with money, power, and a standing army think that people over which they claim to rule *ought* to be a certain way and not another *regardless of their consent or will*, look out!

Lincoln, however, was not trying to convey anything that had to do with the actual meaning or intent of the author of the *Declaration of Independence*. Lincoln only evokes the language of the *Declaration of Independence* in his Address to give his imaginary nation an air of legitimacy. Maybe he meant it this way:

> Negroes have natural rights however, as other men have, although they cannot enjoy them here [Meaning in United States proper, or its territories], and even Taney once said that "the Declaration of Independence was broad enough for all men." But though it does not declare that all men are equal in their attainments or social position, yet no sane man will attempt to deny that the African upon his own soil has all the natural rights that instrument vouchsafes to all mankind. (Emphasis added)

—Abraham Lincoln, 1858[51]

So, they are equal, but just not here. Interesting...

A lot of people have told me that he changed his views on race as the war moved along. I have never seen or read anything to substantiate this, but that's neither here, nor there...

I really don't know, and I really don't care what Lincoln thought or didn't think about 'equality.' It is irrelevant since we know there was no nation in 1776 as he claims.

I have come to know better what Lincoln was and nothing he said shocks me much anymore (almost nothing I thought I knew turned out to be consistent with reality, as far as it can be known and shown, in 'American' History I was taught and once believed—one nation, one history! Confederates were the bad guys!).

All I know that whatever it means or is supposed to mean, it has *nothing* to do with any self-evident truths, at least not verifiably so.

## WHY THE COLONISTS FOUGHT

Jefferson's use of the language of John Locke's theory of abstract human rights,[52] was an unfortunate choice because it distracts readers—particularly post-'Civil War' readers who view the document through the lenses of Mr. Lincoln's address—from the real abuses of power against which the colonists actually fought and against which many died in the act. This is a very important question, but it just isn't really considered outside of soundbites such as 'taxation without representation'—not out of dishonesty in most contemporary cases, in my opinion, but because most people were *neither* taught using the actual primary documents without the post-war nationalist interpretation of the state of affairs *nor* ever considered that America's 'nationhood' is entirely based on Lincoln's

---

51 *The Collected Works of Abraham Lincoln*, ed. Roy R. Basler (New Brunswick, NJ: Rutgers University Press, 1953-1955), vol. 3, p. 80.

52 See Bonus Chapter at the end of the book for all the dirty details...

French-style revolution of 1861-1865 and not *the* Constitution or the rule of law or some noble purpose—it was a war against the States—and not just the Southern ones (the other ones did not find out until later who the new boss was). But I digress...

It was not equality in the abstract to which the colonists were dedicated, they were dedicated of ridding themselves of a King who was in violation of the English Constitution, their colonial charters, and against their inherited and traditional Rights as Englishmen. This had the effect of stripping them of their rightful station in the British Empire by actual offences of/by the King and this was *intolerable.*

Of what was the King guilty? Here's a long list adapted from the text of *The unanimous Declaration of the thirteen united States of America.*[53]

(Now is a good time to grab a drink or some popcorn, take a bathroom break, and find a comfortable seat—this is a very long list, trust me (I typed it)—skip most of it if you must—but this is the real deal as laid forth by the representatives of the colonies, now States in this influential *declaration* Americans claim to cherish.)

The King was guilty of the following:

- By refusing his Assent to Laws, the most wholesome and necessary for the public good,

- By forbidding his Governors to pass Laws of immediate and pressing importance, unless suspended in their operation till his Assent should be obtained; and when so suspended, he utterly neglected to attend to them,

---

53   Try to place these complaints within the context of the preamble to the Declaration. It may be the only way to 'see' what the real problem was, not Lincoln's 'interpretation, which is, well... b.s.!

- By refusing to pass other Laws for the accommodation of large districts of people, unless those people would relinquish the right of Representation in the Legislature, a right inestimable to them and formidable to tyrants only,

- By calling together legislative bodies at places unusual, uncomfortable, and distant from the depository of their public Records, for the sole purpose of fatiguing them into compliance with his measures,

- By dissolving Representative Houses repeatedly, for opposing with manly firmness his invasions on the rights of the people,

- By refusing for a long time, after such dissolutions, to cause others to be elected; whereby the Legislative powers, incapable of Annihilation, were returned to the People at large for their exercise; the State remaining in the meantime exposed to all the dangers of invasion from without, and convulsions within,

- By endeavouring to prevent the population of the States; for that purpose obstructing the Laws for Naturalization of Foreigners; by refusing to pass others to encourage their migrations hither, and raising the conditions of new Appropriations of Lands,

- By obstructing the Administration of Justice, by refusing his Assent to Laws for establishing Judiciary powers,

- By making Judges dependent on his will alone, for the tenure of their offices, and the amount and payment of their salaries,

- By erecting a multitude of New Offices and sending swarms of Officers to harass the people, and eat out their substance,

- By keeping among them, in times of peace, Standing Armies without the Consent of their legislatures,

- By affecting to render the Military independent of and superior to the Civil power,

- By combining with others to subject the colonists to a jurisdiction foreign to their constitution, and unacknowledged by their laws; giving his Assent to their Acts of pretended Legislation,

And for other offences including:

- Quartering large bodies of armed troops among the colonists,

- Protecting these troops, by a mock Trial, from punishment for any Murders which they may commit on the Inhabitants of those States,

- For cutting off their Trade with all parts of the world,

- For imposing Taxes on them without their Consent,

- For depriving them in many cases, of the benefits of Trial by Jury,

- For transporting them beyond Seas to be tried for pretended offences,

- For abolishing the free System of English Laws in a neighbouring Province,[54] establishing therein an Arbitrary government, and enlarging its Boundaries so as to render it at once an example and fit instrument for introducing the same absolute rule into the Colonies,

- For taking away their Charters, abolishing their most valuable Laws, and altering fundamentally the Forms of their Governments,

- For suspending their Legislatures, and declaring themselves invested with power to legislate for them in all cases whatsoever,

- Furthermore, this King abdicated Government in the colonies, by declaring the colonists out of his Protection and waging War against them AND,

---

54   Meaning the recently 'established' government of conquered Quebec.

- Plundering their seas, ravaging their Coasts, burning their towns, and destroying the lives of the people,

- By transporting large Armies of foreign Mercenaries to complete the works of death, desolation and tyranny, already begun with circumstances of Cruelty & perfidy scarcely paralleled in the most barbarous ages, and totally unworthy the Head of a civilized nation,

- By constraining their fellow Citizens taken Captive on the high Seas to bear Arms against their Country, to become the executioners of their friends and Brethren, or to fall themselves by their Hands,

- By exciting domestic insurrections amongst us, and endeavouring to bring on the inhabitants of their frontiers, the merciless Indian Savages, whose known rule of warfare, is an undistinguished destruction of all ages, sexes and conditions.

That's a lot of offences, I'd say...

It's not like the colonists, dear reader, over the course of many years, did not try to smooth things over—they did! Nevertheless, at every stage of their oppressions placed on them by the King and Parliament, the colonists petitioned for redress in the humblest terms: Their repeated petitions being answered only with repeated injury.

They warned their British brethren of attempts by their legislature to extend an unwarrantable jurisdiction over them. They reminded them of the circumstances of their emigration and settlement on the American continent. They appealed to their native justice and magnanimity, and they conjured them by the ties of their common kindred to disavow these usurpations, which, would inevitably interrupt their connections and correspondence.

But they would not listen.

The colonists, therefore, had no choice—if they wanted to maintain their inherited rights which were no longer acknowledged or respected by the only sovereign that they recognised—but to absolve themselves from all allegiance to the British Crown and from all political connection with the State of Great Britain and declare themselves independent States with all of the rights, responsibilities, duties, and obligations that such a state of independence includes...

This I can understand. These are valid reasons to resist arbitrary power, by arms if necessary.

This makes sense.

This requires no abstract theory of rights or how government (in the abstract) came into being.

This is plain, simple; rooted in time and space.

This is what makes the Declaration of Independence, truly, a *declaration of independence* not an explication of the state of mankind and certainly not an 'unfinished work' for these United States to remake the world in its own image or some such.

Because this misunderstood proposition, originating in a philosophical tradition of abstract rights,[55] was plucked out of the Declaration by Lincoln and foisted on the people of America in a clever address which somehow grants unlimited power to the government to accomplish its divine mandate—to make the proposition that 'all men are created equal' true—we have inherited quite a *flocking*[56] mess and it will only get messier as long as people continue to believe it.

---

55  Social Contract Theory. See 'Bonus Chapter' at the end of the book.

56  Not a typo. I promised myself that I would not drop F-bombs in this book.

41

## WHAT ABOUT THE 'CONSENT OF THE GOVERNED'?

If a great man of towering genius (as we are told), Mr. Lincoln, would have read the rest of the passage—assuming his reverence for the Declaration of Independence was genuine, and not a mere prop—there would have been no war, so many senseless deaths, and all the lies built upon this bullshit mythology would be transparent. And you, dear reader, would not be sitting or lying where you are right now reading my quirky 'deconstruction' of the Gettysburg Address because nothing would have caused one to go there and memorialise the thousands who fell in the battles at Gettysburg in the first place.

Why did he stop where he did?

To try and solve this mystery, let us quickly look at the *entire* passage since he only employed the first part of it:

> We hold these truths to be self-evident, that all men are created equal, that they are endowed by their Creator with certain unalienable Rights, that among these are Life, Liberty and the pursuit of Happiness.—That to secure these rights, Governments are instituted among Men, deriving their just powers from the consent of the governed, —*That whenever any Form of Government becomes destructive of these ends, it is the Right of the People to alter or to abolish it, and to institute a new Government, laying its foundation on such principles and organizing its powers in such form, as to them shall seem most likely to affect their Safety and Happiness.* (Emphasis added)

Let's blend the first part and the second part to better understand what is really being said:

- That to secure these rights [i.e., life, liberty and pursuit of happiness], Governments are instituted among Men,

- [These governments] deriving their just powers from the consent of the governed,
- [Because this is why governments are created in the first place—that is, to secure life, liberty and the pursuit of happiness—and where they get their legitimacy—that is, from the consent of the governed...] whenever any Form of Government becomes destructive of these ends, it is the Right of the People to alter or to abolish it.
- [If the latter] to institute new Government, laying its foundation on such principles and organizing its powers in such form, as to *them* shall seem most likely to affect *their* Safety and Happiness. (emphasis added)

I don't know how you get around Lincoln's position on the exodus of the Southern States, given that the point and purpose of *The unanimous Declaration of the thirteen united States of America*, is that any State or collection of States (even Southern ones) may 'alter' or 'abolish' their form of government when it seems to them that a new arrangement is likely to better affect their safety and happiness. The whole point of the passage when read in full—indeed, its *fundamental* and *central* point—is *not* the state of humanity or some new political dogma to be spread with bullets and bombs, but rather it is the liberty of a people to choose—according to their own analysis of the situation, how and by whom they will be governed.

If the colonists were right in 1776, then the Confederates (whether you agree with them or not) were right in 1861. This is the simple fact of the matter, and anyone can understand it if they let their imagination run wild for a moment and consider the possibility. Close your eyes and imagine this happened anywhere but in the South which had slavery both under the laws of their own State and the laws of the Federal Union. It's going to be tough, but go ahead and give this a try:

After freely leaving the Union known as the United States of America in their sovereign capacity as States through a solemn convention of the people of their States, there was another convention of the people in each of the States similarly situated and

43

it was decided that they would join together to create a new union—one which more closely resembled the union they thought they had joined in 1787-1788.

Let us not forget, dear reader, that these same States created and brought into existence *through their free and unfettered ratification as sovereign States*, the *first* union under the Articles of Confederation and a *second* union under the Constitution for The United States.

And yet... and yet... they were *told* by a government, possessing only delegated powers from the States themselves, that they did *not* have the authority and would not be allowed to leave the union created by the second constitution; this *even though they had legally and properly*, according to their own laws, *elected representatives from their 'neck of the woods' to carry their sentiments of the people in their community to the convention then considering a new form of government through yet another American Constitution*: a third American union that came to be known as the Confederate States of America.

This was not some silly mid-term election; this was serious business. And they made their will known by either freely accepting or rejecting the proposed constitution, that is, whether the State would join up with the other States that ratified the document and make a go of it, or stay put. No one held a bayonet at their breast or gun to their head. They did what they thought was in the interest of their State, their home—indeed, their country! You may think it was a bad idea, or that they were motivated by some unwholesome motive, but that changes nothing. If they had the power to do it twice, they had the power to do it three times (or as many times as they wished until they got what they wanted).

How is it that the South is demonised as traitorous or of being 'Un-American' because some of the States of the voluntary union, felt that it was no longer in their interest to remain in a political arrangement that had clearly strayed from the agreement to which they entered; something they had previously done by seceding from the British Empire, and then acceding to the first constitution from which they later seceded by ratifying the second constitution? Were not these same corporate societies able to do the same thing as their fathers and grandfathers had done?

Was not this second Constitution, freely agreed upon by all parties, created for their good and the good of every State, and adopted with the express assurance—both within the 4 corners of the document and the assurances of its proponents, that certain powers were delegated to the Federal or General Government by the States, but mostly retained by them? Was this not the understanding of the people of the several States at their ratification conventions? If so, who or whom, and under what authority, were the terms changed to create a 'national' government from which no State could withdraw?

How can anyone conclude that a State, or a collection of States— given the foregoing—cannot decide for themselves whether or not it is in their interest to separate from a group of very different people, with very different values, *and* who could no longer tolerate one another for reasons real and imagined, should continue to be yoked together when every effort had been made to keep the peace with one another?

They could not even agree upon the nature and purpose of the Union itself when all relevant documents were available to consult what the people of the several States agreed to and what they did not agree to.

If you think *leaving* such a growingly unpleasant situation (putting it mildly) peacefully after legally withdrawing from the Second American Union, was less desirable than what Lincoln did and was doing as he gave the address at Gettysburg—the hundreds of thousands of deaths, senseless destruction to which every American should be ashamed, and a legacy of racial and regional tension (and sometimes violence), up to this very day—then you are one horrifying specimen of humanity. In fact, I would be interested in how you would determine what the acceptable body count to maintain the geographical integrity of THE United States of America and hold an independent people captive.

The very part of the Declaration Lincoln employs in summoning up his 'Proposition Nation' was only the precondition to the overarching point of the passage itself, namely, the consent of the governed, the right of the people to alter or abolish the government, etc.

How did an otherwise intelligent person miss that?

The only reasonable answer that I can conjure is that he *chose* to.

What a very different world this would be if he would have acted judiciously according to the principles expressed in the Declaration of Independence without selective editing.

Together, the two unions could have settled any common debt, the South could reimburse the old Union for any U.S. property residing in the territory of the new federation, arrangements could have been made for trade and travel, and everyone could have gotten back to living their own lives, but 'our greatest president' chose the interest of his political party over the interest of the federation of States.

This made war inevitable.

Few can face what has been done or bring themselves to admit that Lincoln's actions were illegal, immoral, and (saddest of all) unnecessary.

# III.

# A CIVIL WHAT?

'Now we are engaged in a great civil war, testing whether that nation, or any nation so conceived and so dedicated, can long endure...'

**WORDS MATTER** and ideas do, in fact, have consequences.

A 'civil war,' by definition, is a war between two or more parties, each of whom are fighting to control a single government. <u>Everyone knows this</u>, yet the nationalists—heirs of Lincoln's proposition nation—refuse to concede this very basic and incontrovertible linguistic point.

Why?

The conflict over which Mr. Lincoln presided was not a war over who would govern the political cesspool on the banks of the Potomac River (Washington, DC), but rather—and this is the long and short of it—it was a war for independence (that is, government by the consent of the governed) on one side and a war of invasion, conquest, and subjugation on the other. It has been called by one author, and accurately so, A WAR TO PREVENT SOUTHERN

INDEPENDENCE.[57] You may wince at the implication of this plain fact, but the conclusion is unavoidable if the so-called 'founding,' as I have described above, is closer to the truth than this nationalist nonsense.

Because there was *never* a nation conceived in the way described by Lincoln, or dedicated to any abstract proposition such as equality, there was *no* legal or moral justification for Lincoln's invasion of the Southern States.

This bears repeating: *Because there was never a nation conceived in the way described by Lincoln, or dedicated to any abstract proposition such as equality, there was no legal or moral justification for Lincoln's invasion of the Southern States* (period, full stop).

If the political entity created by the Constitution of 1787 actually made a nation, then it could not logically be broken-up. A nation, by definition is *one thing*. However, the *Constitution* did *not* create a *nation*; it created a *union*. A *union*, by contrast is *not* one thing, but a plurality—two or more existing parties joined together by contract or agreement for specific purposes.

## LINCOLN'S ARGUMENT AGAINST SECESSION IN HIS FIRST INAUGURAL ADDRESS

In Lincoln's first inaugural address on 4 March 1861, he lays out his case for the perpetuity of the Union, or Nation—*words he uses interchangeably* in this part of the address.

Although it is not a particularly long passage, it requires a lot of unpacking to see what Lincoln—that cunning linguist and master debater—was doing.

---

57   Charles T. Pace. *Southern Independence—Why War? The War to Prevent Southern Independence* (Columbia, SC: Shotwell Publishing, LLC, 2015).

There is some serious word play in this performance. I will number each statement so that they can be easily referred to in the course of the following analysis of Lincoln's argument against Southern Independence. Read the passage in whole, then we'll slice it and dice it up.

Here you go:

[1] ... I hold that in contemplation of universal law and of the Constitution the Union of these States is perpetual.

[2] Perpetuity is implied, if not expressed, in the fundamental law of all national governments.

[3] It is safe to assert that no government proper ever had a provision in its organic law for its own termination.

[4] Continue to execute all the express provisions of our National Constitution, and the Union will endure forever, [5] it being impossible to destroy it except by some action not provided for in the instrument itself.

[6] Again: If the United States be not a government proper, but an association of States in the nature of contract merely, can it, as a contract, be peaceably unmade by less than all the parties who made it?

[7] One party to a contract may violate it break it, so to speak—but does it not require all to lawfully rescind it?

[8] Descending from these general principles, we find the proposition that in legal contemplation the Union is perpetual is confirmed by the history of the Union itself. [9] The Union is much older than the Constitution. [10] It was formed, in fact, by the Articles of Association in 1774.

[11] It was matured and continued by the Declaration of Independence in 1776.

[12] It was further matured, and the faith of all the then thirteen States expressly plighted and engaged that it should be perpetual, by the Articles of Confederation in 1778.

[13] And finally, in 1787, one of the declared objects for ordaining and establishing the Constitution was 'to form a more perfect Union.'

[14] But if destruction of the Union by one or by a part only of the States be lawfully possible, the Union is less perfect than before the Constitution,

[15] having lost the vital element of perpetuity.

[16] It follows from these views that no State upon its own mere motion can lawfully get out of the Union;

[17] that resolves and ordinances to that effect are legally void, and that acts of violence within any State or States against the authority of the United States are insurrectionary or revolutionary, according to circumstances.

This is going to be a tough nut to crack. There is a lot going on here, so buckle up!

*

The first claim Lincoln makes was that when he contemplates 'universal law'[58] and (not 'or,' but 'and'—meaning *both* of them together) the 'Constitution' he has concluded that the Union (note the word used here: 'Union') is perpetual. [1]

---

58 What is universal law here? I have no idea. Is it Universal Law such as 2 + 2 = 4? Or gravity will pull you to the ground if you jump off the Empire State Building? That kind of law, or something else? He does not say.

How does he arrive at this conclusion?

For the balance of the first section of this address, Mr. Lincoln explains how he arrived at this *general* conclusion by reference to *universal law*. Lincoln refers to the Constitution of 1787 (sort of) with some apparent back and forth between the two pillars on which he rests his case: The document itself and 'universal law.'

He first opens with a universal claim:

> [2] 'Perpetuity is implied, if not expressed, in the fundamental law of all national governments.'

Now, my dear reader, it may very well be the case that the fundamental law governing national governments is that they are perpetual, but the 'Union' has a federal, not national form of government. Lincoln seemingly took it for granted that there was one American people with one form of government—a national one—and the States were like counties—not sovereign bodies that created the institution Lincoln is characterising as national. It should go without saying at this point that this was not the way the States saw each other or themselves when they ratified this second American Constitution. The Southern States and the Southern people, having a long memory, knew what they were, how they got there, and the proper remedy when all other efforts had failed.

(We have already shown—*ad nauseum*—that none of the founding documents created, in any way shape or form, a national, top-down, or centralised government.)

Note again that the words 'union' and 'nation' are used interchangeably, as if they were one and the same thing. In the preceding statement he says that the 'Union of these States is perpetual.' Now he switches to the word 'nation,' saying that perpetuity is a fundamental characterization of a 'national government'—a rhetorical 'bait and switch' manoeuvre.

Continueth Lincoln:

> [3] 'no government proper ever had a provision in its
> organic law for its own termination.'

Presumably, because a national government is 'indivisible,'
we may assume it is a 'government proper,' the implication being
that the actions of the Southern States made the United States
an improper form of government. Of course, it is easily perceived
that this argument is circular, pretending to be an argument from
definition, but it is really a form of equivocation or conflation ideas
by using two words with different meaning as if they were the same
(and clearly they are not).

Did the Southern States destroy the Union or, more importantly
in Lincoln's view, the government of the United States?

Of course not!

The seceding States merely left.

The United States of America and its government still existed
after the Southern exodus and was free to go about its business
without the South getting in the way of all of their grand designs.
You'd think they'd be dancing in the streets to be rid of us, but
Lincoln's false notion of an indivisible nation (sometimes called a
'Union' when it fits his purposes) made this opportunity of a lifetime
impossible.

Statements [4] and [5] take his universal notions and applies
them to the Constitution of 1787:

> [4] Continue to execute all the express provisions of
> our National Constitution, and the Union will endure
> forever,
>
> [5] it being impossible to destroy it except by some
> action not provided for in the instrument itself.

Because Lincoln holds that that these United States are a nation with a national constitution, he doesn't seem to mind that the document to which he refers specifies what the federal government can do and what it cannot do—if, in the Constitution, certain actions or functions are not expressly delegated to the government at Washington, DC, nor prohibited to the States, they are *reserved to the States respectively, or to the people* as per the Tenth Amendment, that amendment nationalists (Left, Right, and anywhere in-between) love to hate.

The Tenth Amendment was added to the constitution of 1787 (in what we now call the 'Bill of Rights') *as a guarantee* to the people of the several States that an all-powerful centralised, that is to say, national, form of government would not and could not arise from this 'more energetic' constitution.

So, to paraphrase the said amendment, let us view the issue through the lenses of the actual document—not some bullshit lawyer or judge's interpretation, which is irrelevant given what we now know—namely, that if the powers to prevent a State from leaving the federation is not delegated to the entity known as the United States by the Second Constitution (and it is not), nor prohibited by the Second Constitution to the States (which it does not), then *the right to leave the Union is reserved to the States respectively, or to the people.*

I don't know how to make the issue clearer.

Secession is not a federal issue and, therefore, the federal authority had no legal right to prevent a State to 'withdraw their consent' for the very reason that it is *not* in the 'instrument itself.'

I know this doesn't sound Constitutional to the modern American ear, but it was the law *then* and is the law *now*, despite what lawyers and judges might say to the contrary. It is to what the States agreed and their agreement, despite scholars, judges, and mythmakers, has never been repealed. There is no American Nation, only a cabal of usurpers who could care less about the union of States or the people of the States, or the rule of law, or anything outside of their normal routine of murder (undeclared wars), theft (taxing the people without their consent to pay for unauthorised expenditures), and coercion (usually through one of the alphabet agencies).[59]

The Constitution of 1787 was passed with the understanding and the assurance that it said what it meant and meant what it said. It is for this reason some States conditionally adopted it with the understanding that a clear and concise 'Bill of Rights' be added as *ample guarantee* that they were not getting involved with a centralized or what we now call a national government. The Tenth Amendment—the last and arguably most important of the ten amendments comprising the Bill of Rights—was instrumental in the States' adoption of the new Constitution. If it was, how do we explain the *conditional* ratification by at least three of the States:

> From the Ratification of the Commonwealth of Virginia:

> We the delegate of the people of Virginia ... Do in the name on behalf of the people of Virginia, declare and make known that the powers granted under the Constitution being derived from the people of the United States, may be resumed by them whensoever the same shall be perverted to their injury or oppression, and that every power not granted thereby remains with them, and at their will ...[60]

> From the Ratification of the State of New York:

> ... the powers of the government may be reassumed by the people whensoever it shall become necessary to their happiness; that every power, jurisdiction,

---

59  I don't like it either. It's pretty damn uncomfortable to say, but I can't see a way around it. I am, therefore, obliged to adopt this seemingly blasphemous position because this is where the argument has led me... and maybe even you.

60  Elliott. *The Debates*, Vol. I, p.250.

and right, which is not by the Constitution clearly delegated to the Congress of the United States, or the departments of the government thereof, remains with the people of the several states, or to their representative state governments, to whom it may be granted the same; and that those clauses in the said Constitution, which declare that Congress shall not have or exercise certain powers, do not imply that Congress is entitled to any power not given by the said Constitution ...[61]

From the Ratification of the State of Rhode Island:

... That the powers of government may be reassumed by the people whensoever it shall become necessary to their happiness. That the rights of the states respectively to nominate and appoint all state officers, and every other power, jurisdiction, and right, which is not by the said Constitution clearly delegated to the Congress of the United States or to the departments of government thereof, remain to the people of the several states, or their respective state governments, to whom they may have granted the same; and that those clauses in the Constitution which declare that Congress shall not have or exercise certain powers, do not imply that Congress is entitled to any powers not given by the said Constitution...[62]

If any of this sounds like the American people in the aggregate acceding to a National Constitution, I'll be damned!

The people of the several States, or their representatives, are the principals to this agreement and the government for the United States

---

61  *Ibid.*, p. 251.

62  *Ibid.*, p. 258.

is their common agent—not in all things whatsoever, but only in those things clearly delegated. Clearly delegated. That was the deal.

There are no implied powers. There is no universal or higher law at play here, neither is there a nation, be it proper or not in Lincoln's view.

> [6] Again: If the United States be not a government proper, but an association of States in the nature of contract merely, can it, as a contract, be peaceably unmade by less than all the parties who made it?

> [7] One party to a contract may violate it—break it, so to speak—but does it not require all to lawfully rescind it?

Other than the rhetorically pregnant word 'merely,' Lincoln perfectly describes the Union as it really is/was, namely, 'an association of States in the nature of contract.' It bears repeating that the Constitution FOR the United States *was the contract that made the government* Lincoln is trying to preserve. The government of the United States is *not a party* to the contract, it is a *creature* of the contract. The *principals* are the States. The government is the *agent* which was authorised to carry out *enumerated* powers delegated by the terms of agreement—nothing more.

Hundreds of thousands of actual people actually died in Mr. Lincoln's war because of this mischaracterisation, and those living under this mis-gendered government today still suffer from the lingering effects of a Federal Union that identified (and continues to identify) as a Nation. Government is supreme over the States (who represent the people) in Lincoln's argument and this is exactly bass-ackward from the Constitution as ratified by the States.

Since we have already seen that the notion of 'government proper' is presented as a characteristic of a national government with a national constitution, and it has not been shown that a national government ever existed, then I think we can safely dismiss this bit of hocus pocus.

The rhetorical questions regarding the consent of the other States—parties to the Constitution—are raised, but not answered. However, the States, as the representative bodies of the people of the States, have no obligation to any other State when it comes to determining the welfare and happiness of their own people.

If *they* (the States or any portion of them) believe that the union is exploiting them or overstepping the enumerated powers and that they are no longer happy with the arrangement, they can and should recall their delegated powers and form a new government which to them seems most likely to affect their safety and happiness.

To clarify this point, I'm going to tell y'all a little story (you know how Southerners love to tell stories), to shed light on what I'm trying to *show* as it relates to Lincoln's 'permission from other States' assertion:

Let us imagine that I contract a company to cut my grass and trim my bushes because I'm busy writing this book and can't get to it myself. Let's call this company... *Mmmmm* ... Let's see ... *uh* ...GOT IT! 'Honest Abe's Lawn Service'

Let us further imagine that Honest Abe's Lawn Service and I agree with one another (contract) that *they* will cut the grass and trim the bushes and I will pay them $150 for this service.

*We agree. They're hired! I sign on the dotted line.*

They are now free to come onto my property and do what I hired them to do.

This state of affairs did not exist before we made this agreement. It was through our agreement that they could be there with the authority, *i.e.* the permission, to do the work. I delegated that authority—it's my yard after all.

Let us continue to imagine that Honest Abe's Lawn Service did their work while I was writing, so I was not there to supervise the work—and why should I have to be there? We have a contract, the terms are set, and I am way behind on my work.

However (*we're still imagining*), when I go outside, I find that *not only* is my grass cut and my bushes trimmed, but new trees and flowers had also been put in.

When I walk over to the supervisor to see what the deal was— we'll call him Stanton—Stanton tells me that I am responsible to pay for all the landscaping they did to my yard.

I respond (obviously) that I'm not going to pay for this. Stanton then retorts, 'The other landscaping was implied.'

To which I reply, 'What do you mean *implied*?'

He says that by hiring Honest Abe's Lawn Service to cut my grass and trim my bushes, I implied that I wanted 'beautification of the yard,' that is, to look better than it previously did. He went on to explain that what they have done makes my yard 'more beautiful' than if they had merely only done the things to which we agreed—for the 'general welfare' of not only my yard, but the neighbourhood itself.

Ok, fine.

Even if it does, I hired this company to cut my grass and trim my bushes—that's it. Nothing further was implied. It was cut and dry, nothing further needed to prove Honest Abe's Lawn Service exceeded their authority—at least that's what you would think in a sane world.

While we can imagine that the yard is beautiful and does, in fact, look better than it would have looked without the trees and flowers, do I owe this company for their loose construction of our agreement?

*Uh... Ha-ail no!* [63]

If other people in the neighbourhood hire them and they do the same thing, are *they* obliged to carry on the relationship? They certainly can if they wish, but I have no obligation to continue my relationship with that company and I don't need to confer with the other households in the neighbourhood who hired this company before I hired them (or after I hired them, it makes no difference).

They all signed up with the company of their own free will and accord, and they can continue that relationship or not. Regardless, I don't have to continue my relationship with Honest Abe's Lawn Service and everyone else, if they don't like it, can suck it! [64] I know what I agreed to, have the paperwork, and no fancy talk can change the plain facts of the case—unless it is by FORCE.

The End.

*

That was a bit long and for that I'm sorry, but the point is this:

Each State that contracted (What else can you call it?) to make the Second American Constitution the law of the land did so *with assurances* that the governing body they were creating would only cut the grass and trim the bushes (to continue the analogy), nothing more. Some of the Southern States called 'bullshit' on the flowers and trees, especially since they had to pay for them (and they did, of course, have to pay for them through internal works and a protective tariff... but that's a story for another day). [65]

---

63  A little dialect writing here. This is the infamous two-syllable Southern rendering of the word 'hell.' You do not want to hear a Southern woman, black or white, direct this two-syllable rendition of 'hell' towards you.

64  What I mean to say is 'they could go about their business and do as they please,' but it just wasn't as good, you know?

65  Think 'Tariff of Abomination' (1828) and the stand-off between President Andrew Jackson and South Carolina. At the time of The War, the Southern states paid 75% (conservatively, I've seen it claimed it was above 80%) of ALL Federal taxes collected. There were no inland taxes or any direct taxes on people by the Washington government at that time.

So, most of the Southern States left the Union, one by one, eventually coming together to form what they believed to be a more perfect union—freely and without coercion.

What's the difference between that and the secession of the States from the Articles of Confederation and their acceding to the U.S. Constitution? None, only Lincoln didn't want it to happen.

But let us continue:

> [8] Descending from these general principles, we find the proposition that in legal contemplation the Union is perpetual is confirmed by the history of the Union itself.

Okay, now Lincoln is back to using the word 'union,' although he has yet to show that 'union' and 'nation' are synonymous, or the government formed under the Constitution of 1787 was a national constitution or created a national form of government.

We all should know by now that it didn't.

Such an idea was expressly rejected by the States.

Next comes a strange whiggish or quasi-Hegelian[66] reading of the history of the colonies/States in America and their relationship

---

It's 'funny' that Lincoln, in his first inaugural, said that he would not invade (i.e., there would be no war) on the account of slavery, that he did not believe he had the authority to do so, AND that he would even support a Constitutional Amendment to make it impossible for the general government to ever interfere with the institution of slavery where it then existed, BUT he would (I'm imagining an image of Mr. Burns of 'The Simpsons'(Homer's boss) rubbing his hands together and giving that wicked grin) collect the taxes and imposts or the war is on. Go read it. Also, if you have a strong stomach, look up 'The Corwin Amendment.' I don't have time in this book to get into this particular issue, i.e., slavery, although it is certainly important for people to know what these documents actually say. See Lincoln's First Inaugural, the Corwin Amendment (ironically, it would have been the 13th amendment), and even the Emancipation Proclamation to see how slavery played a role in the conflict.

66   Whig history is an approach to historiography that presents history as a journey from an oppressive and benighted past to a 'glorious present' (Wikipedia— a poor source, I know—but sufficient for this case). Hegelian history goes a little something like this: 'nature is the embodiment of reason. In the same way that nature strives

to one another. It defies common sense, reason, and a plain reading of the documentary evidence. According to Lincoln (and I assume he said this with a straight face):

[9] The Union is much older than the Constitution.

[10] It was formed, in fact, by the Articles of Association in 1774.

[11] It was matured and continued by the Declaration of Independence in 1776.

[12] It was further matured, and the faith of all the then thirteen States expressly plighted and engaged that it should be perpetual, by the Articles of Confederation in 1778.

If by this he meant that the colonies cooperated with one another in various ways and under various agreements prior to the Constitution of 1787, then sure, but he is using the word Union as if it passed through several progressive stages—'matured,' he says—until it reached perfection under the Second American Constitution.

This is foolishness.

Does a marital union precede, in some mystical way, the bride and the groom? Does it do so in contemplation of 'Universal Law'? Even courtship and engagement does not guarantee a marriage,[67] and even a marriage itself can be dissolved under certain circumstances.

---

towards increasing complexity and harmony, so does the world spirit through the historical process.' (Jack Fox-Williams, 'Hegel's Understanding of History,' *Philosophy Now: A Magazine of Ideas*, Issue 140) at philosophynow.org (accessed 12 December 2023) Quick link: bit.ly/HegelHistoryLink.

67 I was engaged twice before I found the right one. It was a damn good thing that either I or the other party called off the wedding and, hence, a marital union that would have greatly affected our happiness (and not in a good way). When we saw it was not what we both wanted, we were at liberty to dissolve our relationship. Go to a pawn shop and check out all the engagement rings! This is the way the real world works.

[13] And finally, in 1787, one of the declared objects for ordaining and establishing the Constitution was 'to form a more perfect Union.'

[14] But if destruction of the Union by one or by a part only of the States be lawfully possible, the Union is less perfect than before the Constitution,

[15] having lost the vital element of perpetuity.

Lincoln's argument that one of the purposes of the Constitution of 1787 was to create a more perfect union (which is what it says) and that secession, that is 'the destruction of the union' by one or more of the States, makes the union less perfect is a curious one. He seems to be saying that the newer constitution is better ('more perfect') than the old one (The Articles), and yet the newer constitution omits the mention of perpetuity all together. It is not carried over to the new governing document. This being the case, either the constitution of 1787 created a 'less perfect' union by omitting any claim to perpetuity—a 'vital element' in Lincoln's argument—or this is simply rhetorical tomfoolery because it was gone with the wind upon, so to say, the adoption of the Second American Constitution, making the former, not the latter 'more perfect,' if 'perpetuity' makes a governing document better or worse. You can't have it both ways. You can only get where Lincoln is in this hodgepodge of rhetorical sleight of hand by an appeal to some mystically summoned 'universal law' and a gross misreading of a Federal document by claiming it is a national one. It's one or the other, dear reader. Not one of the States united ever agreed to submitting to (1) an undefined 'universal law,' no one (2) ever adopted or ratified a national constitution, and (3) any claim to perpetuity was lost with the adoption of the constitution of 1787.

Jettisoning the old perpetual union, that is, *The Articles of Confederation and perpetual Union [between the States of...]* as sovereign, free, and independent States, shows that the concept of perpetuity is secondary to the express will of the people of the several States (that's who 'We the People' are in the preamble to the Second Constitution).[68]

The 'framers' *could have* expressly stated that the new union was perpetual, but they *didn't*.

*How could they?*

They were attempting to overturn the Federal Constitution of these United States that *claimed to be perpetual*.

They also *could have* called this new form of government 'national,'[69] or something tending to that effect. Many of the 'founding fathers' in attendance at Philadelphia would have loved that, but they *didn't*.

THEY DIDN'T, dear reader, and no judicial hocus pocus or legislative abracadabra can make it read otherwise.

The centralisers lost.

I'm sorry, but they really did.

No State was going to sign on to live under an all-powerful centralised government—and they emphatically, through their Ratification Documents, did not.

But we, dear reader, who are living under a government based on this outrageous assemblage of lies perpetrated by Lincoln and those who followed, are not given the option[70] to choose the government under which we would be governed whenever it seems judicious and in the interest of the people (who are always the people of a State).[71]

---

68   See Appendix D.

69   Or any other centralised form of government which is superior to the people where they work, live, and die.

70   Such as we have seen in other countries like Quebec in Canada, the Scottish Independence referendum in the United Kingdom, and BREXIT with regards to membership in the European Union in recent years.

71   Who are always the people of some place—in the case of these United States—that place is their State. Every ratification of the Second Constitution expressly indicated that they were speaking on behalf of the people of their State—not the other—not the

Instead, we have been blessed—thanks to Lincoln and other nationalist lawyers, judges, and politicians—this three headed-monster we call the Federal Government[72] which claims to be a legitimate government, maintains its existence by fattening its belly with the blood, sweat, and tears of its subjects. America: a life sentence without trial with no chance of parole—forced together and ruled by whoever can acquire 51% of the vote, by fair means or foul. Not just Southerners, but all Americans since the time of Lincoln and, presumably (if they continue to have their way) until Gabriel blows his trumpet and the seven seals are opened; we must continue to live in a faux nation created out of hundreds of thousands of dead bodies, knitted back together with barbed wire and bayonets; a government that currently no longer even *pretends* that the Southern States are a legitimate part of America's history as generations past had at least tried to do.[73]

It all comes down to this:

Would you choose (or anyone you know choose) to live under this government as it is? With no escape, no redress, and no meaningful (if any) representation at the Federal level.[74]

---

people in the abstract or 'individuals' living within the boundaries of a 'nation' the size of a continent. Specific people. People from somewhere.

72   E.g., Because the executive, legislative, and judicial bodies are all part of the same government— 'checks and balances,' in and among themselves, is not possible, especially when ruling on the extent of their own power.

How many of you think a 'Supreme' Court would ever strike down an unconstitutional law, such as Obamacare, The Patriot Act, or the National Defence Authorisation Act (and others too many to name), after having been nominated by the executive branch, confirmed by the Senate, and paid by the House. The cards are stacked, my friends.

73   As of the writing of this book (2023), there has been a big battle going on regarding the 'Reconciliation Monument' located at Arlington Cemetery (Robert E. Lee's stolen land in which they continue to bury soldiers to this very day). This monument was intended to mark the end of the hostilities and personal animosity between the sections engendered by the war of 1861-1865. This reconciliation worked for a while, but it required putting lies on top of lies to maintain the *status quo*. From my simple way of thinking, this is *not* a good formula for promoting and maintaining 'national unity.' I fully expect that the monument will come down... and soon!

Does the removal of the monument mean that the sections are no longer reconciled and the war is back on? (Asking for a friend.)

74   See next chapter.

By falsely describing the American union as a nation, both in his first inaugural address and later in the Gettysburg Address, Mr. Lincoln could call the conflict a civil war without credulity and rhetorically justify holding it together by force. This reasoning, however brilliant, was patently false *then* and is patently false *now*.

# IV.

## Dying in Vain

'...We have come to dedicate a portion of that field, as a final resting place for those who here gave their lives that that nation might live... The brave men, living and dead, who struggled here, have consecrated it, far above our poor power to add or detract. It is for us the living, rather, to be dedicated here to the *unfinished work* which they who fought here have thus far so nobly advanced... [and] gave the last full measure of devotion—that we here highly resolve that *these dead shall not have died in vain...*' (emphasis added)

AFTER RECOUNTING THE MYTHOLOGICAL BIRTH of Lincoln's imaginary nation, we must take courage as we look at the consequences of this false rendering of history. Its legacy is blood, rivers of blood—blood not shed to save a nation, but rather to create one by force of arms; one established without the consent of the governed. Lincoln's words are not only untrue, but they also made (and continue to make) a mockery of the dead that he 'memorialised' in his address. There was <u>no nation to save</u> and, therefore, there is <u>no 'unfinished work'</u> for 'us' or anyone else to continue.

Insofar as the War created a 'nation'—albeit one born in blood and not in law, tradition, or the unfettered consent of the governed, but by force of arms—it also created a mission.

But let us not allow ourselves to obscure the obvious: this mission is *innovation*; it is *revolutionary*; it is ingrained in a false understanding of what *actual* people, at some *actual* time, *actually* said and *actually* did during the period under discussion.

It has nothing whatsoever to do with the cause of 1776 or the union that was created by either the (1) *Articles of Confederation* or the (2) *Constitution for the United States*. This *de facto* nation, but *de jure* criminal cabal (what else can it be called?), has since the subjugation of the South, subjugated every other State of the old Union (and those that came after or may yet come into the 'Union,' nation, or whatever it calls itself these days).

*This could not have happened if the Constitution of 1787, as understood and ratified by the States, was the standard by which we determine laws for the Union.* Imagine George Washington fighting in Europe or any other part of the world—in a 'war to end all wars' or 'to make the world safe for democracy' or any war that did anything other than protect the homeland. You can't make your mind do it! (And he was a Federalist and friend of Hamilton!)

*

Once a swindle of this magnitude (the Gettysburg Address) gets a foothold (and it has) and the fruits of its consequences are brought to light (which they continually are), the guilty party/parties is/are obliged to hide its crimes and bolster their cover story to legitimise their actions under this b.s. national facade.

*The Gettysburg Address is certainly among the most eloquent alibis in history, but it is a false alibi.*

As much as we may wince at the implication of such an assertion, we must not look the other way.

The Union soldiers—note the absence of 'national' in this appellation applied to the US military throughout the war—under Lincoln's command were not holy warriors fighting for either a nation or a proposition (and certainly not to free slaves or anyone else), they were victims of ambition and revolution instigated by the head of a new sectional political party openly hostile to the Southern States and formally pledged against her interests—the Republicans![75]

Those men's blood, those men who lay in the dark, dank earth as Lincoln rattled off that nonsense, only was shed in vain if we refuse to call their slaughter what it was and bravely cast the blame where it belongs! How can 'we' solve anything anywhere if our foundation is a mountain of lies?[76]

I know where to cast the blame during Lincoln's time, but who or whom is to blame for its continuance?

Does this thing we call the Federal Government have anything to do with the American Constitution of 1787? If not, *who* said they could change it? *Who* provided permission to allow judges, lawyers, and politicians to interpret *our own law* and twist it into a grotesque assemblage of implied and/or inferred powers, or just pluck 'rights' out of the air, rights to which no one would freely consent (unless it were to their *direct benefit* and would *not cost them anything*)? Inventing absurdity after absurdity that were never even imagined before we were all hoodooed by that voodoo that they do.[77]

---

75  Our 'conservative' heroes who stand in the breach to protect the regular folk from the designs of the Democrats! Spare me! Q: What exactly have they or do they conserve? A: Nothing! That's why we are in the mess we are in right now. (*May God have mercy on us!*)

76  I want to make it clear that I do not believe most folks raised ('reared,' for our Yankee readers) well after the war were purposefully lying—they did not know; they were taught the falsehood and never had a reason to question what they had been told. I was obliged to question the narrative when I found in my personal studies 'parts' that did not fit. I will be the first to admit that I am still working through how everything fits, but if it cannot fit them all (as far as they are knowable), I can know, however, the narrative is wrong or wrong as it is being presented.

77  No offence meant towards witch doctors, hoodoo practitioners, or believers in such in the audience. I'm pretty sure I did not come up with the phrase on my own. Maybe a song or something? It fit, that's all.

## BUT, BUT, BUT...

I hear someone out there saying, 'How could they know that X, Y, or Z would become an issue at that time?' You are correct (and I fully agree) that they could not, but they did know 'things' may require some shifting about over the course of time and maybe even some big changes would need to be made to the document to accommodate a new situation; hence, they put together an amendment process to address such issues.

If the *Federales* wanted to control—let's just throw something out there—healthcare, for example, such a thing would require an AMENDMENT to delegate such a power to the government at Washington because that power has not been delegated. Until it is delegated, it is not there—not by hook, or by crook, or by any other trick in the book.

Some might say that it is too impractical, to which I respond...

First of all, granting a power affecting *circa* 340 MILLION people ought to be well thought-out, and properly vetted in each of the States, *especially* those that would be impacted by the new power under consideration (at the very minimum). The fact that people 'wait' on the decision of 'the court' to determine the constitutionality of a given issues speaks volumes to our inability to remember who we are and where we came from—this is true for heritage Americans[78] as well as those who have adopted America for their home.

Second, an amendment would be available instantaneously. The States would have it as soon as it passed out of Congress.

We have the internet and devices galore that can send the information online in real time. Worst case scenario, even if the wi-fi was out, the document could be overnighted by one of the many delivery services—the delay in transmission being minimal.

---

78  Descendants of the 'founding' stock who were the beneficiaries of independence.

The States' representatives could debate the merits of this amendment and freely decide whether or not they are willing to delegate this particular power to the central government. It could be live streamed. A referendum or some other method of ascertaining the will of the people of the State could be set into motion.

(The same thing would be true if there were an amendment that originated with a convention of States—things would just move in the other direction.)

The thing would then be done.

No questions.

No problem.

No silly argument before the courts and the feds could proceed, if granted, with the support of the people of the several States—or at least a large majority of them.

*

Maybe someone will say that the States and their people—especially those conservative ones (whatever that means)—would never pass anything 'for the good of the 'nation.'

WHAT are they saying?

That the people and their representatives cannot be trusted to determine what is in their own best interest?

From whence, dear reader, does the authority come if not by constitutional amendment vetted by the will of the people through their representatives?

Yes. Their representatives.

*

I think I hear another voice: 'But, don't we have representation in the U.S. Congress?'

*Great question!*

We will need to take a brief detour, however, to address this very important issue.

## BRIEF DETOUR

Dr. Donald Livingston, Professor of Philosophy (Emeritus) at Emory University, in a speech given at the Ludwig Von Mises Institute[79] made a claim that at first glance seems ridiculous, or at least hyperbole. According to Livingston:

> We no longer enjoy self-government and the rule of law at the national level and the only hope for restoring those things is through the States as units of the federal system.

This is a fairly grim statement—even more grim as we approach the 2024 election season where people are anxious to put their team representative (Team Blue v. Team Red) in some office or other in Washington to 'save' us from the machinations of the opposing team—but he then goes on to point out that this state of affairs is not probable, but true. Just a fact.

I am going to be using his observations, easily verifiable, in this section to bring this travesty to the forefront.

As of January 2023, the total population of these United States was approximately 339,172,809 persons. In 1913, the United States House of Representatives was capped at 435 members which yields a ratio of 1 representative per every 779, 708 persons—a meaningless ratio for the purposes of self-government.

---

79  Donald W. Livingston. 'What is Wrong with the Amendment Process and What Can Be Done About It,' Austrian Scholars Conference, Ludwig Von Mises institute, Auburn, AL, 10 March 2012. Available online at bit.ly/Livingston-LVM-03122012 (Accessed 22 November 2023). Note: I 'borrow' liberally from this speech, but the numbers have been updated to reflect the current population.

To illustrate the absurdity of this ratio, Livingston uses James Madison's ratio of 1 representative per 30,000 persons for comparative purposes. This may or may not be the proper ratio for self-government, but it was what the 'Father of the Constitution' thought was an acceptable ratio.

If we applied Madison's ratio to our current population, we would have 11,305 members of the U.S. House—far too large a number for debating laws or carrying out their legitimate functions without falling all over each other.

To look at it another way, if our current ratio were held at the adoption of the Second American Constitution, the first United States Congress would have had a mere 5 members—clearly too few for self-government for the approximate 4,000,000 persons living at that time.

The problem, argues Livingston, is one of scale—the United States has grown too large for a representative form of government at the Federal level.

But this is not all.

In these United States, it requires only a majority of the Senate, House, and the signature of the President to pass laws that affect the lives of almost 340 million people consists of a mere 269 people (if all members were present and voting plus the President). Most laws, however, are passed by the majority of a 'quorum,' equalling in number to only 135 people.

'Never in Human History,' says Livingston, 'has so much political and financial power been placed in so few hands.' He's right. It hasn't. *Never!*

But it is even worse than that, according to Livingston. Most of the laws under which we live do not come from Congress, as required by the Constitution. They come from the 'bloated bureaucracy' under the control of one person, the president.

It's even worse still:

Most important social policies in the areas of religion, morals, speech, etc., issues reserved to the States per the Second Constitution are decided by 9 judges who rule from the 'Supreme Court,' often at a 5/4 split.

If that's not bad enough for you, the 'Supremes' also exercise 'judicial review,' that is, claim to be the final arbiter on the constitutionality of any law at any and all levels of government, including State and local—a power neither delegated nor implied under the Constitution that created this body. If this is the case, and it is for all intents and purposes, then 'farewell to the rule of law.'

Be sure and write your congressional representative when they go against the wishes of the people of their district. *'Let your voice be heard!'*

I'm sure they'll get right back to you with a message crafted by their own hand and not some form letter created by an intern and signed by an electronic signature machine.

## CONCLUSION

Amendments to the Constitution, as you know from civics class,[80] go to the STATES for ratification.

If the States (each and every one of them included) can make or break an amendment—and they can—then they are not subordinate to the 'national authority,' but its master—it's maker or breaker. This may explain the scarcity of amendments submitted to the States for ratification as is required by the Second American Constitution. They have found a work around that seems to work, at least for now.

The *Federales* somehow convinced the people (and this happened long ago) that nine well-connected lawyers/judges proposed by the President, confirmed by the Senate, and paid by the House, being member of a court under the moniker 'Supreme,' should interpret the Constitution. To put it another way, most of us

---

80   Do they teach that anymore?

now *believe* that a branch of the government created by the Second American Constitution (judiciary, in this case) know what powers were delegated to the government (of which they are a part) by the States *better* than the States themselves? (The States being a representative body, representing the *people* of that State.) Many have come to believe that this branch of the federal government is the final authority.

But is it?

In any case involving the actions or laws or authority of the federal government as it pertains to the constitutional status of such an action, the 'Supreme' Court should recuse itself. It is not a disinterested party (being a creature of the compact).

Question: Would you bring a case against Honest Abe's Lawn service if the judges were employees of said lawn service, or intimates of the owner of the business?

Of course not. Impartiality is impossible in such a scenario. The same is true of the Judiciary branch of the Federal Government.

When did the people of the States united, AKA 'We the people' of the several States ever hand over this kind of authority to this or any other federal court?

If someone out there says, 'What about *Marbury v. Madison?*' they have entirely missed the point of this chapter.

# V.

# A Government Of Some People, By Some People, And For Some People

'... that *this nation*, under God, shall have a new birth of freedom — and that government *of* the people, *by* the people, *for* the people, shall not perish from the earth.' (Emphasis added.)

**THESE ARE, BY FAR**, the most audacious statements of the address!

A new birth of freedom for *whom*? A government of, by, and for *what* people? [81] He doesn't say. It is such a sweeping and grand statement that just about anything (or anyone) could be read into it and normally is.

The Southern States and the Southern people could not be read into this pronouncement, although Lincoln never 'officially' recognised their independence, the legitimacy of their government, or their right to exist—they were *just* 'rogue' States who thought they could leave the Union.

---

81  If you are tempted to say, 'enslaved persons,' I invite you to read *Emancipation Hell* by Kirkpatrick Sale. The issue of slavery and emancipation is outside of the scope of this work, but Sale lays it out chapter and verse (and it's only about 100 pages. Visit ShotwellPublishing.com for more information on this title).

Here's the rub: The Southern States would, in the name of *self-government*, be invaded, sacked, burned, pillaged, raped (both black and white Southern women), and have their region left in utter ruin by Lincoln's army because they had the temerity to assert the right to govern themselves as their fathers had done in 1776 by separation from a Kingdom with whom they could not reconcile AND had done in 1787 when they seceded from the First American Constitution (Articles) to accede to the Second American Constitution—the former being a 'perpetual union' to which they pledged their loyalty and replaced it the only way it could be, namely, by the solemn conventions of the people of each State for themselves and for no one else—freely and without bloodshed.

Why?

It has been said that John C. Calhoun, in response to Andrew Jackson's toast, 'to the Union, it must be preserved,' replied, 'The Union: next to our Liberty the most dear: may we all remember that it can only be preserved by respecting the rights of the States, and distributing equally the benefit and burden of the Union!'

That's the meaning of the whole bloody War and everything surrounding it, boiled down to its bare essence.

That's how the Southern people viewed it, and that's why the Southern States left the Union one by one and then came together to form a new Union—a more perfect union, one might say. If the Southern were anything, they were *PRO-CONSTITUTION* (as ratified). Jefferson Davis begged for a trial. He knew the law, but he was never granted his day in court.[82]

The previous two constitutions were a utilitarian means to an end and that end was not a proposition—it was liberty and self-government—and so was the third American Constitution, namely,

---

82 I highly recommend *Was Davis a Traitor; or Was Secession a Constitutional Right in 1861?* by Albert Taylor Bledsoe (1866). It is available in a few paperback trade editions that are easily accessible. It's a life changing read. You can probably find an online copy. Read at your own peril, this is one of those books that have been known to cause paradigm shifts!

the Constitution for the Confederate States of America, freely and fully adopted by the people of the States so ratifying.

The people of the several Southern States had never been governed without their own consent and never intended to do so. Thus, with the loss of the war, the South—along with the union soldiers who had fallen in the bloodletting of 1861-1865—lost all ties to the principles that animated the spirit of 1776 and that were supposed to be preserved in the First and Second Constitutions, but weren't. Not because the documents were inherently flawed—the CSA Constitution[83] is almost an exact replica of the Constitution of 1787 (but one which closed the loopholes that had been exploited to further centralise the general government while they were in the union)—but because the growing Northern majority took advantage of their numerical superiority to exploit the machinery of government, especially through protective tariffs which benefitted Northern manufacturers and funded internal improvement that were mostly funded by the South through 'protective' tariffs.

Compromises were made over and over in an attempt to mitigate the conflicting interests of the northern and Southern States of the Union, but the election of Lincoln in 1860 showed the South that they would not and could not be co-equal members of the Union with the election of the sectional president Abraham Lincoln and the ascendancy of the Republican Party.

Lincoln did not campaign in the South and did not appear, as far as I can tell, on the ballots of any Southern State.

It was like the toast of President Jackson and Vice-President John C. Calhoun cited above had been made flesh and the political implications of each position was about to play out as it always was going to—or at least this is the way one might see it looking back.

---

83  If you want to know about the kind of society the South was building, that for which they fought, and what it was 'all about,' this is the most obvious and sensible source. It shows plainly the kind of federation the Southern States (by the usual means, i.e., ratification) were fighting to maintain and what they saw as necessary to make the old constitution (II) do what it was supposed to have done, that is, what for which they thought signed up for when they ratified it. Easily found online.

Lincoln won the presidency with 40% of the popular vote. This ended, as history shows, all hope of either reconciliation or a peaceful, negotiated separation between the antagonistic sections.

But let us not view this as a loss to the States of the Confederacy alone, all American States had lost their option to govern themselves when self-determination was lost by brute force alone. The whole thing is a tragedy we see played out almost every day up to our own time, devolving and worsening as every year goes by.

The country we thought we had has long ceased to exist if it ever did. The government—what Lincoln called the 'National Authority'—what we have NOW—is fraudulent government deeply invested in the 'nationalist myth'—an 'indivisible nation' with all of the markings of the post-French Revolutionary Nation-State.[84]

It's not like I'm the only one out there who has noticed that the Gettysburg Address is a less-than-truthful tale spun by Mr. Lincoln.

American journalist, essayist, and magazine editor, H.L. Mencken (1880-1956) pointed out the absurdity of the doctrine expressed in the Gettysburg Address in a 1922 sketch on Lincoln. Mencken's words are as powerful now as they were over 100 years ago:

> Think of the argument in it. Put it into the cold words of everyday. The doctrine is simply this: that the Union soldiers who died at Gettysburg sacrificed their lives to the cause of self-determination – that government of the people, by the people, for the people, should not perish from the earth. It is difficult to imagine anything more untrue. The Union soldiers in the battle actually fought against self-determination; it

---

84  You know, the kind that was sweeping Europe ever since King Louis lost his head and the reign of terror took hold of the French people (most of whom were not French) that was supposedly committed to 'Liberty, Fraternity, and Equality,' but appeared to be more committed to tyranny, force, and the bloody guillotine.

was the Confederates who fought for the right of their people to govern themselves.[85]

One more time:

'The Union soldiers in the battle actually fought against self-determination; it was the Confederates who fought for the right of their people to govern themselves.' Let that sink in for a moment... It is bigger than it appears at first glance.

But wait, there's more:

Lincoln Historian and Pulitzer Prise winner Garry Wills called the Gettysburg Address 'a *giant*, if benign, *swindle*.' (Emphasis added.) Lincoln's words, although *admittedly false*, accomplished a great many things in Mr. Wills's estimation.

It (1) *created* a 'different America' by (2) *clearing* 'the infected atmosphere of American history' and (3) *cleansing* the Constitution. Best of all, for Mr. Wills, Lincoln's words *gave* the American people (some of them, at least) (4) 'a new past to live with that would change their future indefinitely...'[86]

A different America?

Clearing history?

Cleansing the Constitution?

A NEW past?

What kind of talk is this? I don't even know how to describe such an assemblage of nonsense.

The Gettysburg Address was certainly a 'giant swindle,' as Wills observed, but it was most assuredly not 'benign.'

---

85  Mencken, H.L. 'Five Men at Random,' *Prejudices: Third Series*, 1922.

86  Wills, Gary. 'Words That Remade America,' *The Atlantic* (www.TheAtlantic.com), November 23, 2011. (Accessed 26 November 2013)

It was, and still remains, a malignant and cancerous lie—a lie that cost untold numbers of lives, an unaccountable loss of blood and treasure, and worst of all, continues to spread a diseased understanding of America right down to our own day.

Generations of Americans have already and will continue to stumble under the weight of this falsehood. Coupled with the psychological violence that this view of history inflicts.

While some believe this to be a fortunate outcome, it came at the expense of the ability of normal, rational thinking Americans to reasonably ascertain *where* they are and *how* they got there.

That is a problem, my friends!

The whole American cause to *maintain their inherited rights*—first as Englishmen under the royal colonial charters and then as the people of the several sovereign States under two different Federal Constitutions—died along with the soldiers at Gettysburg. In fact, all the dead of the war, civilian and military, and the aftermath of what continues to our very own time when 'liberty and self-government' have been exchanged for a bloated and morbidly obese bureaucratic nightmare that tells us what kind of toilets we can use, what kind of light bulbs we can't use, claims to own our labour by taxing it (they used to call that slavery), tells us that insurance premiums are a 'tax,' and redefines social institutions such as marriage as though they were God almighty! *Who granted them this authority?*

We should all be ashamed to talk about the freedoms we enjoy in this 'nation' of fraud, force, intimidation, and theft—the land of good intentions, unintended consequences, and collateral damage! It's the *government* that is guilty of these things, *not the people* or the land where we live.

*That's 'America'!* That thing in Washington, DC is *not* 'America' (it's also *not* a nation or the government of a nation)!

There are many years and endless examples to back up the correctness of General Robert E. Lee's prediction as to what were to happen to America should it become consolidated into 'one vast republic,' as it did when the Southern Confederacy laid down their arms (foolishly, in my opinion) thinking that The War was (or could ever be) over.[87] In a correspondence with Lord Acton in 1866, Lee surmised that this all-powerful, centralised government being created was sure to be 'aggressive abroad and despotic at home.'[88] I'm not sure a better description of the American Empire (albeit long before it had completely morphed into the Fuster-Cluck we have today), has ever been more accurate.

If you couldn't or wouldn't believe the 'national authority' to be 'that bad' before, the year 2020 (and the attendant mischief—to put it politely) should have left you with no lingering doubts about the nature and capacity of the criminal cabal of the 'rich men [and women] north of Richmond' and like it says in the song, I (really and truly) 'Wish I could just wake up and it not be true, but it is...'[89]

We should know that we can wish all we want, but it won't change a damn thing.

---

87   Remember the toast? These are the issues at the bottom of it all.

88   See 'The Acton-Lee Correspondence [of 1866]' Courtesy of LewRockwell.com. Quick link: bit.ly/lee-acton-1866

89   Oliver Anthony Music, 'Rich Men North of Richmond,' 2023. See: bit.ly/OAM-Rich-men-2023.

# VI.

## AMERICA'S CREATION MYTH

**ADMITTEDLY, WORDS CAN DO A LOT OF THINGS**, but despite their many powers, words *cannot* transform a fib into a fact. They cannot change the past; cannot change the terms of a compact; and they most certainly *cannot create a nation out of thin air*!

Neither the court historians, nor the media, or even the might of the United States government can make the words of the Gettysburg Address correspond to reality (as far as it can be known and documented). They can only perpetuate the lie; guard the lie; and call those who attempt to expose the lie a lot of unflattering names. We may live to see stronger measures for speaking out about the cornerstone of this faux nation and the pack of lies upon which it rests.

This particular lie—at least until recently—seemed relatively secure. Social Justice, Critical Race Theory, and a growing throng of strange post-modern ideologies are trying to replace *this* particular nationalist myth with *another* nationalist myth, equally flawed as it relates to what America is, including, of course, the proposition to which it is supposedly dedicated.

The *1619 Project,* no less than President Trump's *1776 Report,* both suffer from the same derangement—belief in the 'Proposition Nation.'[90]

Both are rooted in a falsification of the plain facts of history readily available to anyone with an internet connection or library card (if they still have books) and a wee bit of time and patience to review the documentary evidence. I know we would like to call upon an expert, or a historian to do the thinking for us, but it ain't necessary. In fact, it is not even preferable. Matters like this demand that you do the work on your own. These documents are in English, in most cases, available in print form, and anyone who has graduated high school—or its equivalent of high school in 1980-somethin'—can read and comprehend what they read. No experience or Ph.D. required. One can look up the meaning of any troublesome word or Latin expression.

Who do you trust?

I would trust YOUR interpretation of the facts as they appear in the historical records regarding the form of government we have over any 'expert' in constitutional law—any day! (I am assuming honesty, of course.)

Unlike other creation myths dismissed out of hand for not having enough evidence, the position I have attempted to articulate has the following items to clearly illustrate the nature of the Union created by the founders under the compact styled the 'Constitution for the United States of America.'

(Note that it is not called the 'Constitution for the *United People* of America,' or 'Constitution for the *United Administrative Political Subdivisions* of America,' or the United *Election Districts* of America, but the 'Constitution for the United *STATES* of America.')

In brief, this is what we have:

---

90  See Brion McClanahan, 'Rejecting the Proposition Nation,' *Chronicles Magazine,* April/May 2021, p. 18ff.

1. The Treaty of Paris in which George, III, recognises each of the former colonies as 'free, sovereign, and independent states.' (see Appendix A)

2. The Articles of Confederation, or the constitution of the confederation of colonies—later States—written during the War for Independence. This provides us with understanding the way the States saw themselves and each other during and after the War for American Independence—the world they still occupied during the ratification process. (see Appendix B)

3. Notes on the 'Constitutional Conventions' by actual participants including Robert Yates's *Secret Proceeding and Debates of the Convention* which was published **34 years** AFTER the event (1821), but conveniently available in reprint editions online and elsewhere; and James Madison's *The Constitutional Convention* first published in 1836, **49 years** AFTER the fact. Also easily found online and elsewhere.

   Both collections offer the reader a peek behind the veil of secrecy that cloaked their creation of a new constitution; you know, the one none of the participants had the authority to create. 'The Constitution for the United States,' (Second American Constitution) as it was sent to the various States, as you might guess at this point, says *nothing* about the creation of a *national* or *centralised* government, neither does it establish a *national mission statement*, including the proposition to which this non-nation is purportedly dedicated—also note that they *had to add* the 'bill of rights' to convince enough opponents of ratification that they were *not* creating a centralised or 'national' governing body by adopting this *new* constitution.

4. The writing of the proponents of the proposed Constitution, the Federalists—why they thought adoption was a good thing and how they argued it. Obviously *The Federalist* by Hamilton, Madison, and Jay, is the most popular collection

of essays explaining the nature, function, and purpose of the *new* government they were proposing with the Second Constitution.

5. The writing of the opponents of the proposed Constitution, the Anti-Federalists (the *real* federalists)—why they thought adoption was a bad thing and how they argued it). Believe it or not, it was not until the 1980s that these works were collected and published! (Wonder why?)[91]

6. The proceedings of the State ratification conventions. See Jonathan Elliot's *The Debates in the Several State Conventions on the Adoption of the Federal Constitution* (commonly called Elliot's Debates).

7. Correspondences and other writings of the participants involved in both the creation and adoption of the Constitution[92];

8. The newspapers and other publications of the time period in question (you can find these online, but sometimes requires a subscription);

9. The arguments on the nature of the Union, for example, the famous Webster-Hayne debates (Available online and in book form) and other debates recorded or written prior to the War to Prevent Southern Independence; and/or

10. Other non-primary sources that straighten things out by employing the kinds of documents I have just enumerated. I will mention two—the best, in my opinion, although there are certainly other worthy candidates for your consideration:

---

91 The book edited by Ralph Ketcham called *The Anti-Federalists and the Constitutional Convention Debates* is mostly recommended given the sheer bulk of the collected work cited above. Part II of the book has some actual speeches by Patrick Henry and other 'Anti-Federalists,' and provides the reader with a pretty good taste of the nature of their opposition to the new federal constitution. It's not the best book, but it beats nothing (which is what most folks have).

92 There is a nice collection here: founders.archives.gov.

    i. Able Upshur's *A Brief Enquiry into the True Nature and Character of Our Federal Government* and

    ii. Albert Taylor Bledsoe's *Is Davis a Traitor: Or Was Secession a Constitutional Right Previous to the War?*.

(Pretend the sentences below are flashing.)

<u>**Warning**</u>**: These books are dangerous paradigm shifters. If you prefer to stay in the U.S. Matrix, so to speak, take the blue pill and stay away from them!**

*

No one has to believe a word I say. It is all documented and easy to access IF the inquirer can remove their nationalist goggles long enough to view the plain facts presented in the documentary evidence without one's Pavlovian conditioning kicking in—one nation, under God, indivisible, one nation, under God, indivisible, one nation, under God, indivisible... This is easier said than done. I know from experience, however...

I once heard it said on good authority that the truth will set you *free.*

I want to get as close to the truth as one can; I also want to be *free.*

I *really* and *truly* hope you do too.

It used to be *THE* American axiomatic position...

# AFTERWORD

**I DO NOT KNOW** where you stand on the Gettysburg Address at this point, but I am convinced, beyond any reasonable doubt, that it is not only nonsense, it is nonsense on stilts![93]

Even more, it is a dangerous falsehood that has somehow acquired the power to alter one's perception of reality—past, present, future—and *not* in a good way!

I'm going to go out on a limb and say that the *real* should take precedence over the *imagined* in matters such as government.)

I may not have it exactly right, but it's closer to being true than the nationalist myth or the myth of the proposition nation in describing where we came from and how we got here.

I'm not sure what one should do with the information I have presented or the information that follows in the appendices, but, I hope it at least helps to re-orient you to what has happened and what is likely to happen if these liars get their way, especially now that the government (and its allies in media, entertainment,

---

93  Phrase coined by Utilitarian philosopher Jeremy Bentham and used to describe the notion of Natural Rights and articulated in Social Contract Theory. I had to put it somewhere because it's the title of the book, right?

and education—to name a few) has become openly hostile to regular folks, as if *they* were the terrorists or some kind of threat to 'our democracy'[94] (or worse) and not themselves.

If nothing else, it is my hope that it will provide a little healthy scepticism and a willingness to question the legitimacy of the powers exercised over us by the government at Washington, DC, who do not represent our interests which are always specific and local.

There are no national issues that need to be addressed because there is no nation.

There is no American people in the aggregate, there are only people who live their lives in a particular place—in these United States, places are located in States.

There is no one-size fits all solution to the problems manifested on this big ole continent.

We don't need to come together under some ideological banner to 'save America.'

There are no national 'issues,' but only issues made national to drive the narrative and make residents of Arizona and Maine feel like they are fellow citizens of *the* United States.

The direction we are travelling under this delusion is not progress, it is the opposite.

My greatest fear (for lack of a better word) is that it will break into thousands of pieces and we will not be prepared to meet the challenges that may very well mean our survival and that of your people (everyone has people, know who yours are—you may need them).

Like Dr. Livingston, I think the answer does, in fact, lay with the States, not because I think they can fix or reform these United States, or can be retooled in some way to 'preserve the union,' but

---

94  I hear this phrase a lot now. I don't know what it means. These United States have never been a democracy. I guess 'the republic' for which the stars and stripes were once said to stand now identifies as a democracy—AKA, mob rule, or three wolves and a lamb voting on what's for supper! (*Lord have mercy!*)

because they are structurally in place and capable of keeping order and organising their communities to keep chaos at bay if (when?) the shite hits the fan.

This can only happen if we carefully select people for local and State offices that love their home more than the geographical expanse folks call America and who are willing to do all in their power to make their communities as self-sufficient as possible. I have food and water in mind here, but also the ability to keep the peace and protect property, and refuse to offer any assistance—and even criminalise, if necessary—any unlawful intrusion by an agent or agents of the federal government into the prerogative of the people of their State (for example, showing up to confiscate guns or some other outrage). We do not have to help them, and we shouldn't. This is not paranoia. Take a look around! We are under no obligation to participate in our own destruction or enslavement and the States have the duty to protect their people.

We are under no obligation to pretend that the nationalist myth portrayed by Lincoln corresponds to reality, in fact we are under an obligation to point out when a falsehood is being presented to ourselves or those around us. This can be done nicely, of course, but being a contributor to a falsehood is not honourable and stains the soul.

It's not my fault that the historical record does not conform to the nationalist myth. They made the myth, I didn't. It's not your fault either and you defend it at your own peril.

It seems to me that the mythmakers ought to be showing where, when, and by what authority this imaginary nation came into being, not me. They are making things up, not me. My reading of the records makes their claims both impossible and dangerous, especially as 'the national authority' has all but committed itself to World War III and this will be a travesty in more ways than one.

Let me make this clear: I make no defence for myself. If I am wrong, I want to know it and I'd be a fool not to examine any evidence that would undercut my argument. I don't want some bullshit flamer contacting me with secondary and tertiary sources, memes, or your opinion on how evil the South was or is. It is irrelevant to the topic. However, if you have a serious and sober rebuttal, I'm totally open to it. You can message me through the Shotwell Publishing website (shotwellpublishing.com) or my personal website (paulcgraham. com).

I'm so grateful that you stayed with me to the end. I hope we can get together again soon—maybe next time you can write the book.

Best wishes,

—Paul

# Appendix A

# Treaty of Paris, Article I (1783)[95]

*Signed on 03 September 1783*

Note: I had intended to include the entire document, but it is very long. I'm mostly interested in the 1st Article which recognises each former colony as 'free, sovereign, and independent States,' and by States, George III means States like France or Spain. You can read the whole thing here: bit.ly/Xtreaty1783. It's an interesting document that goes into great detail concerning the terms of surrender. – PG.

**HIS BRITANNIC MAJESTY** acknowledges the said United States, viz., New Hampshire, Massachusetts Bay, Rhode Island and Providence Plantations, Connecticut, New York, New Jersey, Pennsylvania, Delaware, Maryland, Virginia, North Carolina, South Carolina and Georgia, *to be free sovereign and Independent States* [plural, Emphasis mine]; that he treats with them as such, and for himself his Heirs & Successors, relinquishes all claims to the Government, Propriety, and Territorial Rights of the same and every Part thereof.

---

95   A transcript of the 'Treaty of Paris,' National Archives Website (archives.gov). See bit.ly/Xtreaty1783 (Accessed 15 October 2023)

## COMMENTARY

Please note that each former colony, now State, were named individually AND that they were each declared 'Free Sovern and Independent States' (plural). This is the exact phrase used in the Articles as they describe their position amongst and between the other States, 'Each state retains its sovereignty, freedom, and independence'.

That transfer of sovereignty by King George was explicit and the States have NEVER divested themselves of this status in any way, shape, or form. If this is the case—and it is—that is what the States were at that time and legally remain to this day. Sovereignty can only be relinquished by an explicit act, such as what was done by King George in the Treaty of Paris. If you can find such a transfer of sovereignty, I'll be damned. They *haven't*, but they *have* FORGOTTEN WHO AND WHAT THEY ARE.

The States, in their sovereign capacity, used to stand-up against Washington and for their citizens, but today the States and their elective representatives are mere lap dogs of the criminal cabal north of Richmond.

In this *almost* unbelievable time of tyranny, lawlessness, propaganda, and never-ending lies, perhaps we ought to wake-up the dogs or find a new pack of dogs all together—ones that know how to respond to an inferior overstepping its bounds. Although the States appear to be politically impotent (and, quite frankly, ridiculous), they ain't lap dogs, but rather, as we have seen, are the masters and creators of the creature to whom they give their love, devotion, and fidelity which properly belongs to the people they claim to represent.

The problem, to continue the metaphor, dear reader, is the treats—federal grants, educational funding, social programs, etc. The just don't seem to be able to say no to the treats!

*Where's Cesar Millan (the Dog Whisperer) when you need him?!*[96]

---

96   If this reference is unfamiliar to you, see bit.ly/XDog-Whisperer.

# Appendix B

## ARTICLES OF CONFEDERATION (NOVEMBER 15, 1777)[97]

*RATIFIED ON MARCH 1, 1781*

Note: Since very few of us know much, if anything, about the First American Constitution, I thought it should be included as an appendix. See Appendix C for a quick and easy comparison of some of the differences between this Constitution, and the one that would come about in 1787. – PG

**TO ALL TO WHOM THESE PRESENTS SHALL COME**, we the undersigned Delegates of the States affixed to our Names send greeting.

---

97 Articles of Confederation, November 15, 1777. Available at ConSource.org: shortened URL: www.qrs.ly/ltef7v8 (Accessed 31 December 2022). The full title (which is too long for the table of contents) is, as you know, the 'Articles of Confederation and perpetual Union between the states of New Hampshire, Massachusetts-bay, Rhode Island and Providence Plantations, Connecticut, New York, New Jersey, Pennsylvania, Delaware, Maryland, Virginia, North Carolina, South Carolina and Georgia.'

Articles of Confederation and perpetual Union between the states of New Hampshire, Massachusetts-bay, Rhode Island and Providence Plantations, Connecticut, New York, New Jersey, Pennsylvania, Delaware, Maryland, Virginia, North Carolina, South Carolina and Georgia.

## I.

The Stile of this Confederacy shall be 'The United States of America'.

## II.

Each state retains its sovereignty, freedom, and independence, and every power, jurisdiction, and right, which is not by this Confederation expressly delegated to the United States, in Congress assembled.

## III.

The said States hereby severally enter into a firm league of friendship with each other, for their common defense, the security of their liberties, and their mutual and general welfare, binding themselves to assist each other, against all force offered to, or attacks made upon them, or any of them, on account of religion, sovereignty, trade, or any other pretense whatever.

## IV.

The better to secure and perpetuate mutual friendship and intercourse among the people of the different States in this Union, the free inhabitants of each of these States, paupers, vagabonds, and fugitives from justice excepted, shall be entitled to all privileges and immunities of free citizens in the several States; and the people of each State shall free ingress and regress to and from any other State, and shall enjoy therein all the privileges of trade and commerce, subject to the same duties, impositions, and restrictions as the inhabitants thereof respectively, provided that such restrictions shall not extend so far as to prevent the removal of property imported into any State, to any other State, of which the owner is an inhabitant; provided also that no imposition, duties or restriction shall be laid by any State, on the property of the United States, or either of them.

If any person guilty of, or charged with, treason, felony, or other high misdemeanor in any State, shall flee from justice, and be found in any of the United States, he shall, upon demand of the Governor or executive power of the State from which he fled, be delivered up and removed to the State having jurisdiction of his offense.

Full faith and credit shall be given in each of these States to the records, acts, and judicial proceedings of the courts and magistrates of every other State.

V.

For the most convenient management of the general interests of the United States, delegates shall be annually appointed in such manner as the legislatures of each State shall direct, to meet in Congress on the first Monday in November, in every year, with a power reserved to each State to recall its delegates, or any of them, at any time within the year, and to send others in their stead for the remainder of the year.

No State shall be represented in Congress by less than two, nor more than seven members; and no person shall be capable of being a delegate for more than three years in any term of six years; nor shall any person, being a delegate, be capable of holding any office under the United States, for which he, or another for his benefit, receives any salary, fees or emolument of any kind.

Each State shall maintain its own delegates in a meeting of the States, and while they act as members of the committee of the States.

In determining questions in the United States in Congress assembled, each State shall have one vote.

Freedom of speech and debate in Congress shall not be impeached or questioned in any court or place out of Congress, and the members of Congress shall be protected in their persons from arrests or imprisonments, during the time of their going to and from, and attendence on Congress, except for treason, felony, or breach of the peace.

## VI.

No State, without the consent of the United States in Congress assembled, shall send any embassy to, or receive any embassy from, or enter into any conference, agreement, alliance or treaty with any King, Prince or State; nor shall any person holding any office of profit or trust under the United States, or any of them, accept any present, emolument, office or title of any kind whatever from any King, Prince or foreign State; nor shall the United States in Congress assembled, or any of them, grant any title of nobility.

No two or more States shall enter into any treaty, confederation or alliance whatever between them, without the consent of the United States in Congress assembled, specifying accurately the purposes for which the same is to be entered into, and how long it shall continue.

No State shall lay any imposts or duties, which may interfere with any stipulations in treaties, entered into by the United States in Congress assembled, with any King, Prince or State, in pursuance of any treaties already proposed by Congress, to the courts of France and Spain.

No vessel of war shall be kept up in time of peace by any State, except such number only, as shall be deemed necessary by the United States in Congress assembled, for the defense of such State, or its trade; nor shall any body of forces be kept up by any State in time of peace, except such number only, as in the judgement of the United States in Congress assembled, shall be deemed requisite to garrison the forts necessary for the defense of such State; but every State shall always keep up a well-regulated and disciplined militia, sufficiently armed and accoutered, and shall provide and constantly have ready for use, in public stores, a due number of filed pieces and tents, and a proper quantity of arms, ammunition and camp equipage.

No State shall engage in any war without the consent of the United States in Congress assembled, unless such State be actually invaded by enemies, or shall have received certain advice of a resolution being formed by some nation of Indians to invade such State, and the danger is so imminent as not to admit of a delay till the United

States in Congress assembled can be consulted; nor shall any State grant commissions to any ships or vessels of war, nor letters of marque or reprisal, except it be after a declaration of war by the United States in Congress assembled, and then only against the Kingdom or State and the subjects thereof, against which war has been so declared, and under such regulations as shall be established by the United States in Congress assembled, unless such State be infested by pirates, in which case vessels of war may be fitted out for that occasion, and kept so long as the danger shall continue, or until the United States in Congress assembled shall determine otherwise.

## VII.

When land forces are raised by any State for the common defense, all officers of or under the rank of colonel, shall be appointed by the legislature of each State respectively, by whom such forces shall be raised, or in such manner as such State shall direct, and all vacancies shall be filled up by the State which first made the appointment.

## VIII.

All charges of war, and all other expenses that shall be incurred for the common defense or general welfare, and allowed by the United States in Congress assembled, shall be defrayed out of a common treasury, which shall be supplied by the several States in proportion to the value of all land within each State, granted or surveyed for any person, as such land and the buildings and improvements thereon shall be estimated according to such mode as the United States in Congress assembled, shall from time to time direct and appoint.

The taxes for paying that proportion shall be laid and levied by the authority and direction of the legislatures of the several States within the time agreed upon by the United States in Congress assembled.

## IX.

The United States in Congress assembled, shall have the sole and exclusive right and power of determining on peace and war, except in the cases mentioned in the sixth article — of sending and receiving ambassadors — entering into treaties and alliances, provided that no treaty of commerce shall be made whereby the legislative power of the respective States shall be restrained from imposing such imposts and duties on foreigners, as their own people are subjected to, or from prohibiting the exportation or importation of any species of goods or commodities whatsoever — of establishing rules for deciding in all cases, what captures on land or water shall be legal, and in what manner prizes taken by land or naval forces in the service of the United States shall be divided or appropriated — of granting letters of marque and reprisal in times of peace — appointing courts for the trial of piracies and felonies commited on the high seas and establishing courts for receiving and determining finally appeals in all cases of captures, provided that no member of Congress shall be appointed a judge of any of the said courts.

The United States in Congress assembled shall also be the last resort on appeal in all disputes and differences now subsisting or that hereafter may arise between two or more States concerning boundary, jurisdiction or any other causes whatever; which authority shall always be exercised in the manner following. Whenever the legislative or executive authority or lawful agent of any State in controversy with another shall present a petition to Congress stating the matter in question and praying for a hearing, notice thereof shall be given by order of Congress to the legislative or executive authority of the other State in controversy, and a day assigned for the appearance of the parties by their lawful agents, who shall then be directed to appoint by joint consent, commissioners or judges to constitute a court for hearing and determining the matter in question: but if they cannot agree, Congress shall name three persons out of each of the United States, and from the list of such persons each party shall alternately strike out one, the petitioners beginning, until the number shall be reduced to thirteen; and from that number not less than seven, nor more than nine names as Congress shall direct, shall in the presence of Congress be drawn out by lot, and the persons whose names shall be so drawn or any five of them, shall be commissioners or judges, to hear and finally determine the controversy, so always as a major part of the judges who shall hear the cause shall agree in the determination: and if either party shall neglect to attend at the day appointed, without showing reasons, which Congress shall judge sufficient, or being present shall refuse to strike, the Congress shall proceed to nominate three persons out of each State, and the secretary of Congress shall strike in behalf of such party absent or refusing; and the judgement and sentence of the court to be appointed, in the manner before prescribed, shall be final and conclusive; and if any of the parties shall refuse to submit to the authority of such court, or to appear or defend their claim or cause, the court shall nevertheless proceed to pronounce sentence, or judgement, which shall in like manner be final and decisive, the judgement or sentence and other proceedings being in either case transmitted to Congress, and lodged among the acts of Congress for the security of the parties concerned: provided that every commissioner, before he sits in judgement, shall take an oath to be administered by one of the judges of the supreme or superior court of the State, where the cause shall be tried, 'well and truly to hear and determine the matter in question, according to the best of his judgement, without favor, affection or hope of reward': provided also, that no State shall be deprived of territory for the benefit of the United States.

All controversies concerning the private right of soil claimed under different grants of two or more States, whose jurisdictions as they may respect such lands, and the States which passed such grants are adjusted, the said grants or either of them being at the same time claimed to have originated antecedent to such settlement of jurisdiction, shall on the petition of either party to the Congress of the United States, be finally determined as near as may be in the same manner as is before presecribed for deciding disputes respecting territorial jurisdiction between different States.

The United States in Congress assembled shall also have the sole and exclusive right and power of regulating the alloy and value of coin struck by their own authority, or by that of the respective States — fixing the standards of weights and measures throughout the United States — regulating the trade and managing all affairs with the Indians, not members of any of the States, provided that the legislative right of any State within its own limits be not infringed or violated — establishing or regulating post offices from one State to another, throughout all the United States, and exacting such postage on the papers passing through the same as may be requisite to defray the expenses of the said office — appointing all officers of the land forces, in the service of the United States, excepting regimental officers — appointing all the officers of the naval forces, and commissioning all officers whatever in the service of the United States — making rules for the government and regulation of the said land and naval forces, and directing their operations.

The United States in Congress assembled shall have authority to appoint a committee, to sit in the recess of Congress, to be denominated 'A Committee of the States', and to consist of one delegate from each State; and to appoint such other committees and civil officers as may be necessary for managing the general affairs of the United States under their direction — to appoint one of their members to preside, provided that no person be allowed to serve in the office of president more than one year in any term of three years; to ascertain the necessary sums of money to be raised for the service of the United States, and to appropriate and apply the same for defraying the public expenses — to borrow money, or emit bills on the credit of the United States, transmitting every half-year to the respective States an account of the sums of money so borrowed or emitted — to build and equip a navy — to agree upon the number of land forces, and to make requisitions from each State for its quota, in proportion to the number of white inhabitants in such State; which requisition shall be binding, and thereupon the legislature of each State shall appoint the regimental officers, raise the men and cloath, arm and equip them in a solid-like manner, at the expense of the United States; and the officers and men so cloathed, armed and equipped shall march to the place appointed, and within the time agreed on by the United States in Congress assembled. But if the United States in Congress assembled shall, on consideration of circumstances judge proper that any State should not raise men, or should raise a smaller number of men than the quota thereof, such extra number shall be raised, officered, cloathed, armed and equipped in the same manner as the quota of each State, unless the legislature of such State shall judge that such extra number cannot be safely spread out in the same, in which case they shall raise, officer, cloath, arm and equip as many of such extra number as they judeg can be safely spared. And the officers and men so cloathed, armed, and equipped, shall march to the place appointed, and within the time agreed on by the United States in Congress assembled.

The United States in Congress assembled shall never engage in a war, nor grant letters of marque or reprisal in time of peace, nor enter into any treaties or alliances, nor coin money, nor regulate the value thereof, nor ascertain the sums and expenses necessary for the defense and welfare of the United States, or any of them, nor emit bills, nor borrow money on the credit of the United States, nor appropriate money, nor agree upon the number of vessels of war, to be built or purchased, or the number of land or sea forces to be raised, nor appoint a commander in chief of the army or navy, unless nine States assent to the same: nor shall a question on any other point, except for adjourning from day to day be determined, unless by the votes of the majority of the United States in Congress assembled.

The Congress of the United States shall have power to adjourn to any time within the year, and to any place within the United States, so that no period of adjournment be for a longer duration than the space of six months, and shall publish the journal of their proceedings monthly, except such parts thereof relating to treaties, alliances or military operations, as in their judgement require secrecy; and the yeas and nays of the delegates of each State on any question shall be entered on the journal, when it is desired by any delegates of a State, or any of them, at his or their request shall be furnished with a transcript of the said journal, except such parts as are above excepted, to lay before the legislatures of the several States.

## X.

The Committee of the States, or any nine of them, shall be authorized to execute, in the recess of Congress, such of the powers of Congress as the United States in Congress assembled, by the consent of the nine States, shall from time to time think expedient to vest them with; provided that no power be delegated to the said Committee, for the exercise of which, by the Articles of Confederation, the voice of nine States in the Congress of the United States assembled be requisite.

## XI.

Canada acceding to this confederation, and adjoining in the measures of the United States, shall be admitted into, and entitled to all the advantages of this Union; but no other colony shall be admitted into the same, unless such admission be agreed to by nine States.

## XII.

All bills of credit emitted, monies borrowed, and debts contracted by, or under the authority of Congress, before the assembling of the United States, in pursuance of the present confederation, shall be deemed and considered as a charge against the United States, for payment and satisfaction whereof the said United States, and the public faith are hereby solemnly pleged.

## XIII.

Every State shall abide by the determination of the United States in Congress assembled, on all questions which by this confederation are submitted to them. And the Articles of this Confederation shall be inviolably observed by every State, and the Union shall be perpetual; nor shall any alteration at any time hereafter be made in any of them; unless such alteration be agreed to in a Congress of the United States, and be afterwards confirmed by the legislatures of every State.

And Whereas it hath pleased the Great Governor of the World to incline the hearts of the legislatures we respectively represent in Congress, to approve of, and to authorize us to ratify the said Articles of Confederation and perpetual Union. Know Ye that we the undersigned delegates, by virtue of the power and authority to us given for that purpose, do by these presents, in the name and in behalf of our respective constituents, fully and entirely ratify and confirm each and every of the said Articles of Confederation and perpetual Union, and all and singular the matters and things therein contained: And we do further solemnly plight and engage the faith of our respective constituents, that they shall abide by the determinations of the United States in Congress assembled, on all questions, which by the said Confederation are submitted to them. And that the Articles thereof shall be inviolably observed by the States we respectively represent, and that the Union shall be perpetual.

In Witness whereof we have hereunto set our hands in Congress. Done at Philadelphia in the State of Pennsylvania the ninth day of July in the Year of our Lord One Thousand Seven Hundred and Seventy-Eight, and in the Third Year of the independence of America.

To all to whom these Presents shall come, we the undersigned Delegates of the States affixed to our Names send greeting.

# Appendix C

## DIFFERENCES BETWEEN THE FIRST AND SECOND AMERICAN CONSTITUTIONS[98]

### Levying taxes

Constitution I:        Congress could request States to pay taxes.

Constitution II:       Congress has a delegated right to levy taxes on individuals.

### Federal courts

Constitution I:        No system of federal courts.

Constitution II:       Court system created to deal with issues between citizens, States.

### Regulation of trade

Constitution I:        No provision to regulate interstate trade.

Constitution II:       Congress has the delegated right to regulate trade between States

---

98  This has been adapted from the comparison made in 'The Constitution: The God That Failed (To Liberate Us from Big Government)' by William Buppert. Published on LewRockwell.com on 26 September 2009. Abbreviated link: www,bit.ly/articles-constitution .

## Executive

Constitution I: No executive with power. President of U.S. merely presided over Congress.

Constitution II: Executive branch headed by President who chooses Cabinet and has checks on power of judiciary and legislature.

## Amending document

Constitution I: 13/13 needed to amend the constitution.

Constitution II: 2/3 of both houses of Congress plus 3/4 of state legislatures, or convention of the States.

## Representation of States

Constitution I: Each State received 1 vote regardless of size.

Constitution II: Upper house (Senate) with 2 votes; lower house (House of Representatives) based on population.

## Raising an army

Constitution I: Congress could not draft troops, dependent on states to contribute forces.

Constitution II: Congress can raise an army to deal with military situations.

## Interstate commerce

Constitution I: No control of trade between States.

Constitution II: Interstate commerce controlled by Congress.

## Disputes between States

Constitution I:     Complicated system of arbitration.

Constitution II:    Federal court system to handle disputes.

## Sovereignty

Constitution I:     Sovereignty resides in States.

Constitution II:    Constitution is the supreme law of the land.

## Passing laws

Constitution I:     9/13 States needed to approve legislation.

Constitution II:    50% +1 of both houses plus signature of President.

# Appendix D

## DRAFT OF PREAMBLE TO THE NEW CONSTITUTION OF 1787[99]

Reported By The Committee Of Five, August 6, 1787
(Approved by delegates)

**WE THE PEOPLE** of the States of New Hampshire, Massachusetts, Rhode-Island and Providence Plantations, Connecticut, New York, New Jersey, Pennsylvania, Delaware, Maryland, Virginia North-Carolina, South-Carolina, and Georgia, do ordain, declare, and establish the following Constitution for the Government of Ourselves and our Posterity.

### COMMENTARY

This approved version of the preamble was, according to Madison, given over to a 'committee on style' whose task it was to make sure it was, well, stylistically correct—not a re-write, just going over it one more time to make sure nothing was amiss. Is this what they did? It did and it didn't.

---

99 James Madison's *Notes of the Constitutional Convention*, August 6, 1787. ConSorce.org; Shortened URL: qrs.ly/rsef7uf. (Accessed 31 December 2022)

They could hardly know in advance which States would adopt it, if any, so it would be presumptuous to start naming the participating States before they actually adopted it. Also, these men, having lived under the Articles of Confederation for many years, knew exactly who "the people" were and did not (presumably), see any problem with the way it was re-written.

The people were always the people of a State—not a free floating, unbound, individual among individuals, or the 'American people' in the aggregate. Everyone knew this, but the 'amended' version, which excludes the names of the States who would eventually adopt this new constitution, opened the door to false understanding or interpretation of the instrument and made an entrance for the nationalist who employ 'We the People' as proof of a consolidated American people, something that never was and still isn't.

Since no one knew how the constitution came into being, what was proposed, who proposed it, and the actual sentiments of the participants towards different models of government for decades after the event, it was an easy mistake to make.

After reading Hamilton's preference for a British Style, top-down, all powerful government, his argument for Federalism and limited government in the *Federalist* seems disingenuous, creepy, and duplicitous (as noted earlier in the book). Maybe he changed his mind after his vision of America was rejected, or maybe he saw the passage of the Constitution as a step on obtaining that which he really desired, and so argued for its passage for this reason. (My position.)

Who knows?

All I'm sayin' is that it has all the characteristics of a quiet revolution—the toppling of a government—not accidentally because the Articles could not be amended to meet the issues the new union was facing, but with premeditation—never intending to do what they were commissioned to do!

The very fact that many representatives brought with them new constitutions to be considered to replace the existing constitution is enough to draw such a conclusion. I cannot prove this conclusion definitively, but it certainly fits circumstantially, and fits better than the nationalist version which tries to force the *round* words and actions of the people and events in question into a *square* narrative.

# Appendix E

## PREAMBLE TO THE SECOND AMERICAN CONSTITUTION PRESENTED AND RATIFIED

**WE THE PEOPLE** of the United States, in Order to form a more perfect Union, establish Justice, insure domestic Tranquility, provide for the common defence, promote the general Welfare, and secure the Blessings of Liberty to ourselves and our Posterity, do ordain and establish this Constitution for the United States of America.

### COMMENTARY

Given what we know, that is, who the United States are and who the people (always from one of the States) are, there really is nothing in this trimmed down version that suggests there is one American people in the aggregate or a national style constitution.

I can't count the number of times I have heard people argue for the nationalist interpretation by employing 'We the people' by which they mean 'We the people of the United States,' which means there is one American people and, *ergo*, America is a Nation (in so many words).

Maybe it's nothing, but given the composition of the Committee on Style, to include the biggest proponent of massive centralisation, Alexander Hamilton, and other Federalists, my Spidey-senses start to tingle.

The participants in the 'Convention' all knew that they did not adopt a national or even centralist form of government and not one shred of evidence in either the writings of the Federalists (centralisers), or the Anti-Federalists (anti-centralisers), or the notes taken by participants in the 'Convention,' or the records of the States's ratification conventions say or even infer anything to the contrary. Don't believe me? Go read them.

The country we thought we had turns out to be a house of cards built on a sandy shore with a hurricane ever looming in the horizon.

Revolutionary actions, like the creation of a nation by force of arms and the 're-imagining' of the simple and documented facts of the founding generation carry with them the seeds of their own demise. Truth will out. Maybe not today, tomorrow, or 100 years from now, but it will eventually crumble despite all the reinforcements that have been deployed to keep the lie from crashing to the ground. This has happened to every empire and will happen to the American Empire birthed by Abraham Lincoln's war against self-government and the rule of law.

# Appendix F

# THE SECOND AMERICAN CONSTITUTION AS PRESENTED AND RATIFIED

Note: Imagine that you are viewing this document for the very first time. It will not be easy, but try to block out all the internal chatter, imbedded preconceptions, and go for it! Do we live under the rule of law if this constitution is the measuring-stick of legitimate Federal legislation? Asking for a friend. (Spelling, grammar, and punctuation follows the original.) – PG

**WE THE PEOPLE** of the United States, in Order to form a more perfect Union, establish Justice, insure domestic Tranquility, provide for the common defence, promote the general Welfare, and secure the Blessings of Liberty to ourselves and our Posterity, do ordain and establish this Constitution for the United States of America.

## Article. I.

### Section. 1.

All legislative Powers herein granted shall be vested in a Congress of the United States, which shall consist of a Senate and House of Representatives.

## Section. 2.

The House of Representatives shall be composed of Members chosen every second Year by the People of the several States, and the Electors in each State shall have the Qualifications requisite for Electors of the most numerous Branch of the State Legislature.

No Person shall be a Representative who shall not have attained to the Age of twenty five Years, and been seven Years a Citizen of the United States, and who shall not, when elected, be an Inhabitant of that State in which he shall be chosen.

Representatives and direct Taxes shall be apportioned among the several States which may be included within this Union, according to their respective Numbers, which shall be determined by adding to the whole Number of free Persons, including those bound to Service for a Term of Years, and excluding Indians not taxed, three fifths of all other Persons. The actual Enumeration shall be made within three Years after the first Meeting of the Congress of the United States, and within every subsequent Term of ten Years, in such Manner as they shall by Law direct. The Number of Representatives shall not exceed one for every thirty Thousand, but each State shall have at Least one Representative; and until such enumeration shall be made, the State of New Hampshire shall be entitled to chuse three, Massachusetts eight, Rhode-Island and Providence Plantations one, Connecticut five, New-York six, New Jersey four, Pennsylvania eight, Delaware one, Maryland six, Virginia ten, North Carolina five, South Carolina five, and Georgia three.

When vacancies happen in the Representation from any State, the Executive Authority thereof shall issue Writs of Election to fill such Vacancies.

The House of Representatives shall chuse their Speaker and other Officers; and shall have the sole Power of Impeachment.

## Section. 3.

The Senate of the United States shall be composed of two Senators from each State, chosen by the Legislature thereof, for six Years; and each Senator shall have one Vote.

Immediately after they shall be assembled in Consequence of the first Election, they shall be divided as equally as may be into three Classes. The Seats of the Senators of the first Class shall be vacated at the Expiration of the second Year, of the second Class at the Expiration of the fourth Year, and of the third Class at the Expiration of the sixth Year, so that one third may be chosen every second Year; and if Vacancies happen by Resignation, or otherwise, during the Recess of the Legislature of any State, the Executive thereof may make temporary Appointments until the next Meeting of the Legislature, which shall then fill such Vacancies.

No Person shall be a Senator who shall not have attained to the Age of thirty Years, and been nine Years a Citizen of the United States, and who shall not, when elected, be an Inhabitant of that State for which he shall be chosen.

The Vice President of the United States shall be President of the Senate, but shall have no Vote, unless they be equally divided.

The Senate shall chuse their other Officers, and also a President pro tempore, in the Absence of the Vice President, or when he shall exercise the Office of President of the United States.

The Senate shall have the sole Power to try all Impeachments. When sitting for that Purpose, they shall be on Oath or Affirmation. When the President of the United States is tried, the Chief Justice shall preside: And no Person shall be convicted without the Concurrence of two thirds of the Members present.

Judgment in Cases of Impeachment shall not extend further than to removal from Office, and disqualification to hold and enjoy any Office of honor, Trust or Profit under the United States: but the Party convicted shall nevertheless be liable and subject to Indictment, Trial, Judgment and Punishment, according to Law.

## Section. 4.

The Times, Places and Manner of holding Elections for Senators and Representatives, shall be prescribed in each State by the Legislature thereof; but the Congress may at any time by Law make or alter such Regulations, except as to the Places of chusing Senators.

The Congress shall assemble at least once in every Year, and such Meeting shall be on the first Monday in December, unless they shall by Law appoint a different Day.

## Section. 5.

Each House shall be the Judge of the Elections, Returns and Qualifications of its own Members, and a Majority of each shall constitute a Quorum to do Business; but a smaller Number may adjourn from day to day, and may be authorized to compel the Attendance of absent Members, in such Manner, and under such Penalties as each House may provide.

Each House may determine the Rules of its Proceedings, punish its Members for disorderly Behaviour, and, with the Concurrence of two thirds, expel a Member.

Each House shall keep a Journal of its Proceedings, and from time to time publish the same, excepting such Parts as may in their Judgment require Secrecy; and the Yeas and Nays of the Members of either House on any question shall, at the Desire of one fifth of those Present, be entered on the Journal.

Neither House, during the Session of Congress, shall, without the Consent of the other, adjourn for more than three days, nor to any other Place than that in which the two Houses shall be sitting.

## Section. 6.

The Senators and Representatives shall receive a Compensation for their Services, to be ascertained by Law, and paid out of the Treasury of the United States. They shall in all Cases, except Treason, Felony and Breach of the Peace, be privileged from Arrest during their Attendance at the Session of their respective Houses, and in going to and returning from the same; and for any Speech or Debate in either House, they shall not be questioned in any other Place.

No Senator or Representative shall, during the Time for which he was elected, be appointed to any civil Office under the Authority of the United States, which shall have been created, or the Emoluments whereof shall have been encreased during such time; and no Person holding any Office under the United States, shall be a Member of either House during his Continuance in Office.

## Section. 7.

All Bills for raising Revenue shall originate in the House of Representatives; but the Senate may propose or concur with Amendments as on other Bills.

Every Bill which shall have passed the House of Representatives and the Senate, shall, before it become a Law, be presented to the President of the United States; If he approve he shall sign it, but if not he shall return it, with his Objections to that House in which it shall have originated, who shall enter the Objections at large on their Journal, and proceed to reconsider it. If after such Reconsideration two thirds of that House shall agree to pass the Bill, it shall be sent, together with the Objections, to the other House, by which it shall likewise be reconsidered, and if approved by two thirds of that House, it shall become a Law. But in all such Cases the Votes of both Houses shall be determined by yeas and Nays, and the Names of the Persons voting for and against the Bill shall be entered on the Journal of each House respectively. If any Bill shall not be returned by the President within ten Days (Sundays excepted) after it shall have been presented to him, the Same shall be a Law, in like Manner as if he had signed it, unless the Congress by their Adjournment prevent its Return, in which Case it shall not be a Law.

Every Order, Resolution, or Vote to which the Concurrence of the Senate and House of Representatives may be necessary (except on a question of Adjournment) shall be presented to the President of the United States; and before the Same shall take Effect, shall be approved by him, or being disapproved by him, shall be repassed by two thirds of the Senate and House of Representatives, according to the Rules and Limitations prescribed in the Case of a Bill.

## Section. 8.

The Congress shall have Power To lay and collect Taxes, Duties, Imposts and Excises, to pay the Debts and provide for the common Defence and general Welfare of the United States; but all Duties, Imposts and Excises shall be uniform throughout the United States;

To borrow Money on the credit of the United States;

To regulate Commerce with foreign Nations, and among the several States, and with the Indian Tribes;

To establish an uniform Rule of Naturalization, and uniform Laws on the subject of Bankruptcies throughout the United States;

To coin Money, regulate the Value thereof, and of foreign Coin, and fix the Standard of Weights and Measures;

To provide for the Punishment of counterfeiting the Securities and current Coin of the United States;

To establish Post Offices and post Roads;

To promote the Progress of Science and useful Arts, by securing for limited Times to Authors and Inventors the exclusive Right to their respective Writings and Discoveries;

To constitute Tribunals inferior to the supreme Court;

To define and punish Piracies and Felonies committed on the high Seas, and Offences against the Law of Nations;

To declare War, grant Letters of Marque and Reprisal, and make Rules concerning Captures on Land and Water;

To raise and support Armies, but no Appropriation of Money to that Use shall be for a longer Term than two Years;

To provide and maintain a Navy;

To make Rules for the Government and Regulation of the land and naval Forces;

To provide for calling forth the Militia to execute the Laws of the Union, suppress Insurrections and repel Invasions;

To provide for organizing, arming, and disciplining, the Militia, and for governing such Part of them as may be employed in the Service of the United States, reserving to the States respectively, the Appointment of the Officers, and the Authority of training the Militia according to the discipline prescribed by Congress;

To exercise exclusive Legislation in all Cases whatsoever, over such District (not exceeding ten Miles square) as may, by Cession of particular States, and the Acceptance of Congress, become the Seat of the Government of the United States, and to exercise like Authority over all Places purchased by the Consent of the Legislature of the State in which the Same shall be, for the Erection of Forts, Magazines, Arsenals, dock-Yards, and other needful Buildings;— And

To make all Laws which shall be necessary and proper for carrying into Execution the foregoing Powers, and all other Powers vested by this Constitution in the Government of the United States, or in any Department or Officer thereof.

## Section. 9.

The Migration or Importation of such Persons as any of the States now existing shall think proper to admit, shall not be prohibited by the Congress prior to the Year one thousand eight hundred and eight, but a Tax or duty may be imposed on such Importation, not exceeding ten dollars for each Person.

The Privilege of the Writ of Habeas Corpus shall not be suspended, unless when in Cases of Rebellion or Invasion the public Safety may require it.

No Bill of Attainder or ex post facto Law shall be passed.

No Capitation, or other direct, Tax shall be laid, unless in Proportion to the Census or enumeration herein before directed to be taken.

No Tax or Duty shall be laid on Articles exported from any State.

No Preference shall be given by any Regulation of Commerce or Revenue to the Ports of one State over those of another: nor shall Vessels bound to, or from, one State, be obliged to enter, clear, or pay Duties in another.

No Money shall be drawn from the Treasury, but in Consequence of Appropriations made by Law; and a regular Statement and Account of the Receipts and Expenditures of all public Money shall be published from time to time.

No Title of Nobility shall be granted by the United States: And no Person holding any Office of Profit or Trust under them, shall, without the Consent of the Congress, accept of any present, Emolument, Office, or Title, of any kind whatever, from any King, Prince, or foreign State.

## Section. 10.

No State shall enter into any Treaty, Alliance, or Confederation; grant Letters of Marque and Reprisal; coin Money; emit Bills of Credit; make any Thing but gold and silver Coin a Tender in Payment of Debts; pass any Bill of Attainder, ex post facto Law, or Law impairing the Obligation of Contracts, or grant any Title of Nobility.

No State shall, without the Consent of the Congress, lay any Imposts or Duties on Imports or Exports, except what may be absolutely necessary for executing it's inspection Laws: and the net Produce of all Duties and Imposts, laid by any State on Imports or Exports, shall be for the Use of the Treasury of the United States; and all such Laws shall be subject to the Revision and Controul of the Congress.

No State shall, without the Consent of Congress, lay any Duty of Tonnage, keep Troops, or Ships of War in time of Peace, enter into any Agreement or Compact with another State, or with a foreign Power, or engage in War, unless actually invaded, or in such imminent Danger as will not admit of delay.

## Article. II.

### Section. 1.

The executive Power shall be vested in a President of the United States of America. He shall hold his Office during the Term of four Years, and, together with the Vice President, chosen for the same Term, be elected, as follows

Each State shall appoint, in such Manner as the Legislature thereof may direct, a Number of Electors, equal to the whole Number of Senators and Representatives to which the State may be entitled in the Congress: but no Senator or Representative, or Person holding an Office of Trust or Profit under the United States, shall be appointed an Elector.

The Electors shall meet in their respective States, and vote by Ballot for two Persons, of whom one at least shall not be an Inhabitant of the same State with themselves. And they shall make a List of all the Persons voted for, and of the Number of Votes for each; which List they shall sign and certify, and transmit sealed to the Seat of the Government of the United States, directed to the President of the Senate. The President of the Senate shall, in the Presence of the Senate and House of Representatives, open all the Certificates, and the Votes shall then be counted. The Person having the greatest Number of Votes shall be the President, if such Number be a Majority of the whole Number of Electors appointed; and if there be more than one who have such Majority, and have an equal Number of Votes, then the House of Representatives shall immediately chuse by Ballot one of them for President; and if no Person have a Majority, then from the five highest on the List the said House shall in like Manner chuse the President. But in chusing the President, the Votes shall be taken by States, the Representation from each State having one Vote; A quorum for this Purpose shall consist of a Member or Members from two thirds of the States, and a Majority of all the States shall be necessary to a Choice. In every Case, after the Choice of the President, the Person having the greatest Number of Votes of the Electors shall be the Vice President. But if there should remain two or more who have equal Votes, the Senate shall chuse from them by Ballot the Vice President.

The Congress may determine the Time of chusing the Electors, and the Day on which they shall give their Votes; which Day shall be the same throughout the United States.

No Person except a natural born Citizen, or a Citizen of the United States, at the time of the Adoption of this Constitution, shall be eligible to the Office of President; neither shall any Person be eligible to that Office who shall not have attained to the Age of thirty five Years, and been fourteen Years a Resident within the United States.

In Case of the Removal of the President from Office, or of his Death, Resignation, or Inability to discharge the Powers and Duties of the said Office, the Same shall devolve on the Vice President, and the Congress may by Law provide for the Case of Removal, Death, Resignation or Inability, both of the President and Vice President, declaring what Officer shall then act as President, and such Officer shall act accordingly, until the Disability be removed, or a President shall be elected.

The President shall, at stated Times, receive for his Services, a Compensation, which shall neither be encreased nor diminished during the Period for which he shall have been elected, and he shall not receive within that Period any other Emolument from the United States, or any of them.

Before he enter on the Execution of his Office, he shall take the following Oath or Affirmation:—"I do solemnly swear (or affirm) that I will faithfully execute the Office of President of the United States, and will to the best of my Ability, preserve, protect and defend the Constitution of the United States."

### Section. 2.

The President shall be Commander in Chief of the Army and Navy of the United States, and of the Militia of the several States, when called into the actual Service of the United States; he may require the Opinion, in writing, of the principal Officer in each of the executive Departments, upon any Subject relating to the Duties of their respective Offices, and he shall have Power to grant Reprieves and Pardons for Offences against the United States, except in Cases of Impeachment.

He shall have Power, by and with the Advice and Consent of the Senate, to make Treaties, provided two thirds of the Senators present concur; and he shall nominate, and by and with the Advice and Consent of the Senate, shall appoint Ambassadors, other public Ministers and Consuls, Judges of the supreme Court, and all other Officers of the United States, whose Appointments are not herein otherwise provided for, and which shall be established by Law: but the Congress may by Law vest the Appointment of such inferior Officers, as they think proper, in the President alone, in the Courts of Law, or in the Heads of Departments.

The President shall have Power to fill up all Vacancies that may happen during the Recess of the Senate, by granting Commissions which shall expire at the End of their next Session.

## Section. 3.

He shall from time to time give to the Congress Information of the State of the Union, and recommend to their Consideration such Measures as he shall judge necessary and expedient; he may, on extraordinary Occasions, convene both Houses, or either of them, and in Case of Disagreement between them, with Respect to the Time of Adjournment, he may adjourn them to such Time as he shall think proper; he shall receive Ambassadors and other public Ministers; he shall take Care that the Laws be faithfully executed, and shall Commission all the Officers of the United States.

## Section. 4.

The President, Vice President and all civil Officers of the United States, shall be removed from Office on Impeachment for, and Conviction of, Treason, Bribery, or other high Crimes and Misdemeanors.

## Article. III.

### Section. 1.

The judicial Power of the United States, shall be vested in one supreme Court, and in such inferior Courts as the Congress may from time to time ordain and establish. The Judges, both of the supreme and inferior Courts, shall hold their Offices during good Behaviour, and shall, at stated Times, receive for their Services, a Compensation, which shall not be diminished during their Continuance in Office.

### Section. 2.

The judicial Power shall extend to all Cases, in Law and Equity, arising under this Constitution, the Laws of the United States, and Treaties made, or which shall be made, under their Authority;— to all Cases affecting Ambassadors, other public Ministers and

Consuls;—to all Cases of admiralty and maritime Jurisdiction;— to Controversies to which the United States shall be a Party;—to Controversies between two or more States;— between a State and Citizens of another State,—between Citizens of different States,— between Citizens of the same State claiming Lands under Grants of different States, and between a State, or the Citizens thereof, and foreign States, Citizens or Subjects.

In all Cases affecting Ambassadors, other public Ministers and Consuls, and those in which a State shall be Party, the supreme Court shall have original Jurisdiction. In all the other Cases before mentioned, the supreme Court shall have appellate Jurisdiction, both as to Law and Fact, with such Exceptions, and under such Regulations as the Congress shall make.

The Trial of all Crimes, except in Cases of Impeachment, shall be by Jury; and such Trial shall be held in the State where the said Crimes shall have been committed; but when not committed within any State, the Trial shall be at such Place or Places as the Congress may by Law have directed.

## Section. 3.

Treason against the United States, shall consist only in levying War against them, or in adhering to their Enemies, giving them Aid and Comfort. No Person shall be convicted of Treason unless on the Testimony of two Witnesses to the same overt Act, or on Confession in open Court.

The Congress shall have Power to declare the Punishment of Treason, but no Attainder of Treason shall work Corruption of Blood, or Forfeiture except during the Life of the Person attainted.

## Article. IV.

### Section. 1.

Full Faith and Credit shall be given in each State to the public Acts, Records, and judicial Proceedings of every other State. And the Congress may by general Laws prescribe the Manner in which such Acts, Records and Proceedings shall be proved, and the Effect thereof.

## Section. 2.

The Citizens of each State shall be entitled to all Privileges and Immunities of Citizens in the several States.

A Person charged in any State with Treason, Felony, or other Crime, who shall flee from Justice, and be found in another State, shall on Demand of the executive Authority of the State from which he fled, be delivered up, to be removed to the State having Jurisdiction of the Crime.

No Person held to Service or Labour in one State, under the Laws thereof, escaping into another, shall, in Consequence of any Law or Regulation therein, be discharged from such Service or Labour, but shall be delivered up on Claim of the Party to whom such Service or Labour may be due.

## Section. 3.

New States may be admitted by the Congress into this Union; but no new State shall be formed or erected within the Jurisdiction of any other State; nor any State be formed by the Junction of two or more States, or Parts of States, without the Consent of the Legislatures of the States concerned as well as of the Congress.

The Congress shall have Power to dispose of and make all needful Rules and Regulations respecting the Territory or other Property belonging to the United States; and nothing in this Constitution shall be so construed as to Prejudice any Claims of the United States, or of any particular State.

## Section. 4.

The United States shall guarantee to every State in this Union a Republican Form of Government, and shall protect each of them against Invasion; and on Application of the Legislature, or of the

Executive (when the Legislature cannot be convened) against domestic Violence.

## Article. V.

The Congress, whenever two thirds of both Houses shall deem it necessary, shall propose Amendments to this Constitution, or, on the Application of the Legislatures of two thirds of the several States, shall call a Convention for proposing Amendments, which, in either Case, shall be valid to all Intents and Purposes, as Part of this Constitution, when ratified by the Legislatures of three fourths of the several States, or by Conventions in three fourths thereof, as the one or the other Mode of Ratification may be proposed by the Congress; Provided that no Amendment which may be made prior to the Year One thousand eight hundred and eight shall in any Manner affect the first and fourth Clauses in the Ninth Section of the first Article; and that no State, without its Consent, shall be deprived of its equal Suffrage in the Senate.

## Article. VI.

All Debts contracted and Engagements entered into, before the Adoption of this Constitution, shall be as valid against the United States under this Constitution, as under the Confederation.

This Constitution, and the Laws of the United States which shall be made in Pursuance thereof; and all Treaties made, or which shall be made, under the Authority of the United States, shall be the supreme Law of the Land; and the Judges in every State shall be bound thereby, any Thing in the Constitution or Laws of any State to the Contrary notwithstanding.

The Senators and Representatives before mentioned, and the Members of the several State Legislatures, and all executive and judicial Officers, both of the United States and of the several States, shall be bound by Oath or Affirmation, to support this Constitution; but no religious Test shall ever be required as a Qualification to any Office or public Trust under the United States.

## Article. VII.

The Ratification of the Conventions of nine States, shall be sufficient for the Establishment of this Constitution between the States so ratifying the Same.

The Word, "the," being interlined between the seventh and eighth Lines of the first Page, The Word "Thirty" being partly written on an Erazure in the fifteenth Line of the first Page, The Words "is tried" being interlined between the thirty second and thirty third Lines of the first Page and the Word "the" being interlined between the forty third and forty fourth Lines of the second Page.

Attest William Jackson Secretary

done in Convention by the Unanimous Consent of the States present the Seventeenth Day of September in the Year of our Lord one thousand seven hundred and Eighty seven and of the Independance of the United States of America the Twelfth In witness whereof We have hereunto subscribed our Names,

G°. Washington

Presidt and deputy from Virginia

> Another Note: I'm sure the States received a copy without the errata, attests, and such, but this was the proposed constitution that came out of Philadelphia and I've never heard of any post-convention changes being made. I did leave off the signatures of the delegates at the convention. If it is of interest, just about any online copy of the document or its appearance in any book includes the signatures. – PG

# Appendix G

## THE SECOND AMERICAN CONSTITUTION AS AMENDED

Note: The following amendments, what are often called the 'Bill of Rights,' which were demanded by some States that needed some reassurance that their prerogatives and traditional rights—rights for which their brothers, fathers, cousins, and sons had recently died, would not be infringed by this federal compact.

Americans already had these rights—that's what they fought the British to protect—they wanted ample guarantee that some new tyrannical government would not infringe upon their inherited and hard-won rights like King George tried to do.

That's the context. Of course, lawyers, judges, and that horror they created with 'case law' or 'legal precedent' makes us blind to what the Second American Constitution actually means and actually says. This is not dense language, as we have been told. Pretend that your State agreed to ratify the constitution of 1787, after much debate and (at times) a slim margin of passage. This puts further restrictions on the agent of the States (AKA, the United States) and its language is clear. – PG

# TRANSCRIPTION

### Amendment I

Congress shall make no law respecting an establishment of religion, or prohibiting the free exercise thereof; or abridging the freedom of speech, or of the press; or the right of the people peaceably to assemble, and to petition the Government for a redress of grievances.

### Amendment II

A well regulated Militia, being necessary to the security of a free State, the right of the people to keep and bear Arms, shall not be infringed.

### Amendment III

No Soldier shall, in time of peace be quartered in any house, without the consent of the Owner, nor in time of war, but in a manner to be prescribed by law.

### Amendment IV

The right of the people to be secure in their persons, houses, papers, and effects, against unreasonable searches and seizures, shall not be violated, and no Warrants shall issue, but upon probable cause, supported by Oath or affirmation, and particularly describing the place to be searched, and the persons or things to be seized.

### Amendment V

No person shall be held to answer for a capital, or otherwise infamous crime, unless on a presentment or indictment of a Grand Jury, except in cases arising in the land or naval forces, or in the

Militia, when in actual service in time of War or public danger; nor shall any person be subject for the same offence to be twice put in jeopardy of life or limb; nor shall be compelled in any criminal case to be a witness against himself, nor be deprived of life, liberty, or property, without due process of law; nor shall private property be taken for public use, without just compensation.

## Amendment VI

In all criminal prosecutions, the accused shall enjoy the right to a speedy and public trial, by an impartial jury of the State and district wherein the crime shall have been committed, which district shall have been previously ascertained by law, and to be informed of the nature and cause of the accusation; to be confronted with the witnesses against him; to have compulsory process for obtaining witnesses in his favor, and to have the Assistance of Counsel for his defence.

## Amendment VII

In Suits at common law, where the value in controversy shall exceed twenty dollars, the right of trial by jury shall be preserved, and no fact tried by a jury, shall be otherwise re-examined in any Court of the United States, than according to the rules of the common law.

## Amendment VIII

Excessive bail shall not be required, nor excessive fines imposed, nor cruel and unusual punishments inflicted.

## Amendment IX

The enumeration in the Constitution, of certain rights, shall not be construed to deny or disparage others retained by the people.

## Amendment X

The powers not delegated to the United States by the Constitution, nor prohibited by it to the States, are reserved to the States respectively, or to the people.

## COMMENTARY

Who shall make NO LAW?

CONGRESS shall make no law!

*Congress* has *no authority* over and has *no say* regarding these enumerated items (and others not *specifically delegated.* See Amendment X).

- They *cannot* establish religion.

- They *cannot* prohibit the free exercise of religion.

- They *cannot* make laws that abridge or limit free speech.

- They *cannot* make laws having anything to do with the press in whatever form it may take (there are no exceptions provided here, including what they now call 'hate speech').

- They *cannot* prevent the people from peacefully assembling for any reason, even if they consider it a bad one.

- They *cannot* deprive the people of the member States the right of petitioning or redressing their grievances to their common agent, the Federal Government.

It is FORBIDDEN!

*That was the agreement.*

If they wanted to have a say in any of these matters, *the Constitution would have to be amended* so that those powers not delegated can be delegated (or not) by the people of the sovereign States.

The courts cannot grant these powers to the general government (via the 'incorporation doctrine' or some other legal absurdity) because they were never expressly delegated those powers.

The only way for the courts to get something that they don't have is to ask for it from the only entities capable of granting it—the States.

# Appendix H

# THE VIRGINIA AND KENTUCKY RESOLUTIONS (1798)[100]

By Thomas Jefferson and James Madison

Note: These resolutions were a response to the 'Alien and Sedition Acts' enacted under the presidency of John Adams. Essentially, these 'laws' constrained the activities of foreign residents and *limited freedom of speech and of the press when it was critical of the president or the government.* You do not need to be a Political Scientist to see that it is in direct violation of the First Amendment of the Constitution of 1787 which states that 'CONGRESS SHALL MAKE NO LAW [and they did in this case] respecting an establishment of religion, or prohibiting the free exercise thereof; or ABRIDGING THE FREEDOM OF SPEECH, OR OF THE PRESS; or the right of the people peaceably to assemble, and TO PETITION THE GOVERNMENT FOR A REDRESS OF GRIEVANCES. (emphasis mine)

---

100 See bit.ly/VA-KY-Resolutions.

## THE VIRGINIA RESOLUTION:

RESOLVED, That the General Assembly of Virginia, doth unequivocally express a firm resolution to maintain and defend the Constitution of the United States, and the Constitution of this State, against every aggression either foreign or domestic, and that they will support the government of the United States in all measures warranted by the former.

That this assembly most solemnly declares a warm attachment to the Union of the States, to maintain which it pledges all its powers; and that for this end, it is their duty to watch over and oppose every infraction of those principles which constitute the only basis of that Union, because a faithful observance of them, can alone secure it's existence and the public happiness.

That this Assembly doth explicitly and peremptorily declare, that it views the powers of the federal government, as resulting from the compact, to which the states are parties; as limited by the plain sense and intention of the instrument constituting the compact; as no further valid that they are authorized by the grants enumerated in that compact; and that in case of a deliberate, palpable, and dangerous exercise of other powers, not granted by the said compact, the states who are parties thereto, have the right, and are in duty bound, to interpose for arresting the progress of the evil, and for maintaining within their respective limits, the authorities, rights and liberties appertaining to them.

That the General Assembly doth also express its deep regret, that a spirit has in sundry instances, been manifested by the federal government, to enlarge its powers by forced constructions of the constitutional charter which defines them; and that implications have appeared of a design to expound certain general phrases (which having been copied from the very limited grant of power, in the former articles of confederation were the less liable to be misconstrued) so as to destroy the meaning and effect, of the particular enumeration which necessarily explains and limits the general phrases; and so as to consolidate the states by degrees, into one sovereignty, the obvious tendency and inevitable consequence of which would be, to transform the present republican system of the United States, into an absolute, or at best a mixed monarchy.

That the General Assembly doth particularly protest against the palpable and alarming infractions of the Constitution, in the two late cases of the "Alien and Sedition Acts" passed at the last session of Congress; the first of which exercises a power no where delegated to the federal government, and which by uniting legislative and judicial powers to those of executive, subverts the general principles of free government; as well as the particular organization, and positive provisions of the federal constitution; and the other of which acts, exercises in like manner, a power not delegated by the constitution, but on the contrary, expressly and positively forbidden by one of the amendments thererto; a power, which more than any other, ought to produce universal alarm, because it is levelled against that right of freely examining public characters and measures, and of free communication among the people thereon, which has ever been justly deemed, the only effectual guardian of every other right.

That this state having by its Convention, which ratified the federal Constitution, expressly declared, that among other essential rights, "the Liberty of Conscience and of the Press cannot be cancelled, abridged, restrained, or modified by any authority of the United States," and from its extreme anxiety to guard these rights from every possible attack of sophistry or ambition, having with other states, recommended an amendment for that purpose, which amendment was, in due time, annexed to the Constitution; it would mark a reproachable inconsistency, and criminal degeneracy, if an indifference were now shewn, to the most palpable violation of one of the Rights, thus declared and secured; and to the establishment of a precedent which may be fatal to the other.

That the good people of this commonwealth, having ever felt, and continuing to feel, the most sincere affection for their brethren of the other states; the truest anxiety for establishing and perpetuating the union of all; and the most scrupulous fidelity to that constitution, which is the pledge of mutual friendship, and the instrument of mutual happiness; the General Assembly doth solemenly appeal to the like dispositions of the other states, in confidence that they will concur with this commonwealth in declaring, as it does hereby declare, that the acts aforesaid, are unconstitutional; and that the necessary and proper measures will be taken by each, for co-operating with this state, in maintaining the Authorities, Rights, and Liberties, referred to the States respectively, or to the people.

That the Governor be desired, to transmit a copy of the foregoing Resolutions to the executive authority of each of the other states, with a request that the same may be communicated to the Legislature thereof; and that a copy be furnished to each of the Senators and Representatives representing this state in the Congress of the United States.

*Agreed to by the Senate, December 24, 1798.*

## THE KENTUCKY RESOLUTION:
### RESOLUTIONS IN GENERAL ASSEMBLY

THE representatives of the good people of this commonwealth in general assembly convened, having maturely considered the answers of sundry states in the Union, to their resolutions passed at the last session, respecting certain unconstitutional laws of Congress, commonly called the alien and sedition laws, would be faithless indeed to themselves, and to those they represent, were they silently to acquiesce in principles and doctrines attempted to be maintained in all those answers, that of Virginia only excepted. To again enter the field of argument, and attempt more fully or forcibly to expose the unconstitutionality of those obnoxious laws, would, it is apprehended be as unnecessary as unavailing.

We cannot however but lament, that in the discussion of those interesting subjects, by sundry of the legislatures of our sister states, unfounded suggestions, and uncandid insinuations, derogatory of the true character and principles of the good people of this commonwealth, have been substituted in place of fair reasoning and sound argument. Our opinions of those alarming measures of the general government, together with our reasons for those opinions, were detailed with decency and with temper, and submitted to the discussion and judgment of our fellow citizens throughout the Union. Whether the decency and temper have been observed in the answers of most of those states who have denied or attempted to obviate the great truths contained in those resolutions, we have now only to submit to a candid world. Faithful to the true principles of the federal union, unconscious of any designs to disturb the harmony of that Union, and anxious only to escape the fangs of despotism, the good people of this commonwealth are regardless of censure or calumniation.

Least however the silence of this commonwealth should be construed into an acquiescence in the doctrines and principles advanced and attempted to be maintained by the said answers, or least those of our fellow citizens throughout the Union, who so widely differ from us on those important subjects, should be deluded by the expectation, that we shall be deterred from what we conceive our duty; or shrink from the principles contained in those resolutions: therefore.

RESOLVED, That this commonwealth considers the federal union, upon the terms and for the purposes specified in the late compact, as conducive to the liberty and happiness of the several states: That it does now unequivocally declare its attachment to the Union, and to that compact, agreeable to its obvious and real intention, and will be among the last to seek its dissolution: That if those who administer the general government be permitted to transgress the limits fixed by that compact, by a total disregard to the special delegations of power therein contained, annihilation of the state governments, and the erection upon their ruins, of a general consolidated government, will be the inevitable consequence: That the principle and construction contended for by sundry of the state legislatures, that the general government is the exclusive judge of the extent of the powers delegated to it, stop nothing short of despotism; since the discretion of those who adminster the government, and not the constitution, would be the measure of their powers: That the several states who formed that instrument, being sovereign and independent, have the unquestionable right to judge of its infraction; and that a nullification, by those sovereignties, of all unauthorized acts done under colour of that instrument, is the rightful remedy: That this commonwealth does upon the most deliberate reconsideration declare, that the said alien and sedition laws, are in their opinion, palpable violations of the said constitution; and however cheerfully it may be disposed to surrender its opinion to a majority of its sister states in matters of ordinary or doubtful policy; yet, in momentous regulations like the present, which so vitally wound the best rights of the citizen, it would consider a silent acquiesecence as highly criminal: That although this commonwealth as a party to the federal compact; will bow to the laws of the Union, yet it does at the same time declare, that it will not now, nor ever hereafter, cease to oppose in a constitutional manner, every attempt from what quarter soever offered, to violate that compact:

AND FINALLY, in order that no pretexts or arguments may be drawn from a supposed acquiescence on the part of this commonwealth in the constitutionality of those laws, and be thereby used as precedents for similar future violations of federal compact; this commonwealth does now enter against them, its SOLEMN PROTEST.

*Approved December 3rd, 1799.*

# Appendix I

## SELECTIONS FROM
## *A POLITICAL CATECHISM* (1830)[101]

By Maria Pinckney

*Question—What do we understand by the Federal Union?*

*Answer—*It is an agreement between Sovereign States, to forbear exerting their sovereign power over certain defined objects, and to exert jointly their sovereign power over other specified objects, through the agency of a General Government. Each State agrees to exert its full sovereign power jointly, for all external purposes; and separately, for all internal purposes, or State concerns.

*Q. Where is this Agreement found?*

*A.* In the bond of Union, or compact between the States, called the Federal Constitution.

---

101 This is a selection from Maria Pinckney's *The Quintessence of Long Speeches, Arranged as a Political Catechism* (Charleston, S.C.: A. E. Miller, 1830). Miss Pinckney was the daughter of Charles Cotesworth Pinckney who, among other things, was a delegate from South Carolina to the Philadelphia Convention in 1787. Thanks to Joe Wolverton for providing a copy of this document. I first read it in his book *What Degree of Madness?: Madison's Method to Make America STATES Again* (Columbia, SC: Shotwell Publishing, 2020). It's worth reading.

*Q. What is the nature of the Federal Constitution?*

**A.** It is a compact based upon cautious and jealous specifications. The distinguished body of men who framed it, guarded and defined every power that was to be exercised through the agency of the General Government—and every other power not enumerated in the compact, was to be reserved and exercised by the States.

*Q. Did the States, in forming the Constitution, divest themselves of any part of their Sovereignty?*

**A.** Of not a particle. The individuality and sovereign personality of the States was not at all impaired. The States agreed, by the Constitution, that they would unite in exerting their powers, therein specified and defined, for the purpose and objects therein designated, and through the agency of the machinery therein created; but the power exercised by the functionaries of the General Government, is not *inherent* in them, but in the States whose agents they are. The Constitution is their Power of Attorney, to do certain acts; and contains, connected with their authority to act, their letter of instruction, as to the manner in which they shall act.

They are the Servants. The power which gives validity to their acts is in their Masters—the States.

*Q. Where is the power of Congress during the recess of that body?*

**A.** It possesses no sovereign power—it is but the agent of the Sovereign States.

*Q. Can you illustrate this retention of Sovereignty by the States by any other example?*

**A.** Suppose an individual, for instance, was to stipulate to transact a portion of his business by an agent, and the remainder by himself, and to forbear to exert his moral faculties, and physical energies upon that class of subjects, which, by his agreement, are to be acted upon by his agent. Has he by his stipulation lessened, impaired, or diminished his moral or physical powers? On the contrary, the validity of the agency depends upon his retaining those faculties, for if he shall become insane, or die, the agent cannot act, because the power of his principal has become extinct; so it is the power, the full subsisting Sovereign Power of the States, which gives validity to the acts of the General Government. The validity of these acts does not result from the exercise of a portion of the Sovereign Power of each State.

*Q. Why then has it been supposed by some, that when the States formed the Constitution, they cut the Sovereignty of each State into two parts, and gave much the larger portion to the General Government?*

A. Many erroneous and mischievous opinions proceed from ignorance of the true meaning of words. Sovereignty, Rebellion, Nullification, &c. we hear every day used, without any precise idea being attached to their signification.

*Q. What is the meaning of Sovereignty?*

A. It is the will of civil society in the Social Compact, which society is a moral person, whose will, like the will of the human being, cannot be divided without destroying the person; we can conceive the will operating in a thousand various ways, but we cannot conceive its separation onto parts; neither can we conceive of the separation of Sovereignty—its unity and life are inseparable.

*Q. How do you define Rebellion?*

A. It is the resistance of an *inferior* to the lawful authority of a *superior*. A child may rebel against a parent—a slave against his master—citizens against the government, and colonies against the mother-country—but a State cannot rebel; because one Sovereign cannot rebel against another, for all Sovereigns are equal. The Sovereignty of the little State of Delaware is equal to that of New-York, or of Russia, though the physical power of those Sovereignties are vastly different. The supposition, therefore, that a Sovereign

State can commit Rebellion,[102] Treason, or any crime whatever, is utterly inadmissible in the science of politics. The idea of crime cannot exist where there is no conceivable or possible tribunal, before which the culprit could be arraigned and convicted. Still less can any State be supposed to incur the guilt of rebellion or treason, by resisting an unconstitutional law of the General Government. The General Government is the creature of the States—the offspring of their Sovereign Power. Is the Creator to be governed by the lawless authority of the Creature? We cannot invert the rule of reason and of law upon that subject, and say, that the superior incurs guilt by resisting the inferior, and not the inferior by resisting the superior.

*Q. What is the meaning of Nullification?*

A. It is the veto[103] of a Sovereign State on an unconstitutional law of Congress.

*Q. Are not unconstitutional laws, of course, null and void?*

A. Undoubtedly; and an act of Usurpation is not obligatory; it is not law, and resistance is justifiable. In virtue of her Sovereignty, the State is the judge of her own rights, and bound as Sovereign to protect her citizens, which she does by nullifying[104] the obnoxious law, and releasing them from any obligation to obey it.

---

102 *Rebel.*—Was a State Government to nullify even a *Constitutional* law of Congress, it could not place the State (that is the people of the State) in an attitude of rebellion; if war ensues, it is one government warring against another, as England against France, &c.   The essence of Rebellion is inferiority.

103 Veto.—A writer in one of the Gazettes says, that Veto is suspensive and Nullification is destructive. It is to be hoped that the late Veto of the President was not meant to be suspensive, but will prove altogether destructive.

104 Nullifying.—It is contended that the Kentucky and Virginia Resolutions, which confirm the right of Nullification, in cases of a palpable, deliberate, and dangerous usurpation of power, speak of resistance by the mode pointed out in them, always in the plural number. That it is the *States* which are bound to interpose; and that, consequently, a *State*, being in the singular number cannot interfere and act individually. This is a mere evasion of the enemies of State Rights; for example: If it were said that the submission or alarm-men were permitted to reveal the secret, by which the heterogenous, spurious party obtained the late victory; is it inferred that they are all to assemble together to avail themselves of the permission, and that one *alarmist*, being in the singular number, cannot, individually, divulge it? It is the individuality and sovereign personality of the State which confers the right of Nullification.

*Q. Has not this right of the State been denied?*

*A.* Only by those who are enemies of State Rights, whose subterfuge is, that they can find Nullification no where in the Constitution. Suppose a State was to make a treaty with a foreign government, to coin money, to grant letters of marque, or assume any power that she had by the compact delegated to the General Government. When Congress should nullify the assumption, would the State have any right to complain that she could not find Nullification in the Constitution. If the implied right is reciprocal, the State possesses the double right to Nullify, for all rights are reserved to her, that are not specified in the Constitution.

*Q. Is there no other check upon the General Government, than the one just mention of Nullification?*

*A.* The oath, the several legislative, executive and judicial officers of the several States take to support the Federal Constitution, ought to be as effectual security against the usurpation of the General Government, as it is against the encroachments of the State Governments. For the increase of the powers by usurpation, is as clearly a violation of the Federal Constitution, as a diminution of these powers by private encroachments; and that oath obliges the officers of the several States as vigorously to oppose the one as the other.

*Q. Could then any collision arise between the States and the Federal Government, were each confined to its proper sphere?*

*A.* The Constitution has left them sufficient space to move harmoniously together; but it is the General Government that is continually wandering out of the sphere of its legitimacy, and usurping powers, that the combined wisdom of the States imagined, they had carefully guarded from all encroachments.

*Q. Have the States ever resumed any of the powers they have delegated to the General Government?*

*A.* Never, in a single instance, have they violated, or attempted the Constitution. The enemies of State Rights pretend, that had the States the right to judge of an unconstitutional law of Congress, (in other words, of an infringement on their Sovereignty) they would transcend their appropriate sphere, and usurp[105] the powers assigned to the General Government. On the contrary, it is not the interest of the States to resume the powers they have delegated. The same motives which led to the formation of the Union, a conviction of its utility, are as strong now that its beneficial effects have been experienced, as when they were only anticipated. They have evinced from the period of its formation, no sentiment so strong, as an ardent and devoted attachment to the Union. In Union, they take their high station among the nations of the earth; and in Union, the Star Spangled Banner waves over every sea. But there is a principle we should never forget, that the greatest good when perverted becomes the greatest evil. The Union as it was formed—an Union of Free, Sovereign and Independent States— and Union, affording equal protection and mutual benefit to all, will be considered the greatest political good; but as highly as it ought to be valued, it is not the greatest possible good. There is one still better—still more precious—one which is prized infinitely higher—it is **LIBERTY**—that **LIBERTY** for which our Fathers toiled and bled. The usurpations and tyranny of Great Britain were not resisted, that the **COLONIES** might be **FREE**, and for the **PEOPLE to be FREE**, the **STATES** must be **FREE**. Whenever the States cease to maintain their Sovereignty unimpared, and become vassals of the General Government. The duration of the Union will then, indeed, be problematical. It is, therefore, on the friends of the State Rights—on the supporters of State Rights—on those who cling to State Rights, as to the palladium of their liberties, that we must rely for the maintenance and perpetuity of the Union,

---

105 Usurp.—All power to govern is delegated or usurped. The delegated power may *Usurp* other powers not delegated, but the power that delegates cannot *Usurp*, it *resumes* the power it has delegated—delegated power is trust. The Trustees, therefore, that is the General Government, *Usurp*. The States, who granted the trust, *resume*.

and not on the enemies of State Rights.[5] The weak—the timid—the apathetic, and the ambitious, who raise the cry of disunion to palsy the unity of usurpation—these are the real disunionsists, and to these and these *only*, will be attributed, the evils arising from the dissolution of the Union.

# Bonus Chapter:

# SOCIAL CONTRACT THEORY
# AND MR. LINCOLN'S 'PROPOSITION'

Note: This is a basic, sketch of Social Contract Theory and its implications. I believed its inclusion in the main body of the text would have been laborious and unnecessary for the purposes of this book.

I think, however, that its consideration is worth the time and effort to read it if you want to (1) understand from whence Jefferson's language in *The Declaration* came and what the language of the relevant part of the preamble discussed above actually means and (2) whether you accept or reject Jefferson/Locke's position—understanding the meaning of the passages in a broader context is worth knowing to round out one's study of the document.

## SOCIAL CONTRACT THEORY

**IN ITS MOST BASIC FORM**, a social contract is a postulated agreement between individuals living in a *state of nature* and a governing power in which some personal liberties are surrendered or, better yet, exchanged for the advantages of living in a well-organised or well governed society. Although this concept can be traced back to ancient Greece, it is not held to be a historical event by most theorists, but is merely a hypothetical prerequisite to justify the authority of some form of collective governance.

While Locke is clearly the inspiration for the preamble to the Declaration, it is the view of the author (who taught this topic to college students for a number of years) that one cannot fully appreciate or understand Locke's version of the Social Contract, especially the 'lingo,' without first knowing Thomas Hobbes—the father of modern Social Contract Theory—which sets up the basic categories and assumptions of the theory employed by Locke.

## HOBBES AND THE STATE OF NATURE

Hobbes held in his magnum opus, *Leviathan*, that the justification of the state is grounded in the 'fact' that without it, we would find ourselves in a *State of Nature* where life is less than ideal—in fact it is famously described by Hobbes as being 'solitary, poor, nasty, brutish, and short.'

Hobbes does not claim that the *state of nature* ever existed in history—it is a *Thought Experiment* that leads to his adoption of the Social Contract theory.

How does he get there?

The fundamental premise for Hobbes is that *ALL MEN **ARE** EQUAL*:

> Nature hath made men so equal in the faculties of body and mind as that, though there be found one man sometimes manifestly stronger in body or of quicker mind than another, yet when all is reckoned together the difference between man and man is not so considerable as that one man can thereupon claim to himself any benefit to which another may not pretend as well as he. For as to the strength of body,

the weakest has strength enough to kill the strongest, either by secret machination or by confederacy with others that are in the same danger with himself.

Even the strongest have to sleep sometime and the weakest could easily murder him in his sleep, so we are all *equal* in our ability to kill or steal from our neighbour.

Hobbes also holds that men are basically equal in abilities of mind.

And as to the faculties of the mind...I find yet a greater equality amongst men than that of strength. For prudence is but experience, which equal time equally bestows on all men in those things they equally apply themselves unto.

This equality leads to instability, anxiety, and fear.

Again, *equality* in this view is something to *escape*, not a social or political ideal.

This is because out of *Equality of Ability* comes *Equality of Hope* in attaining one's end. Any two individuals desiring the same thing which they both cannot have, therefore, become rivals or enemies.

This separates men *who are not social creatures by nature* in Hobbes's view, from bees and ants which are social creatures that seem to cooperate without any coercion. Thus, for Hobbes, *the individual precedes society*.

It is important to note the revolutionary nature of Hobbes's position: prior to Hobbes, in fact, for most of human history, people *were* viewed as social creatures (or animals) and never as individuals *only*. It was their natural state.

Aristotle, in *Politics*, summarizes this understanding as follows:

> Man is by nature a social animal; an individual who is unsocial naturally and not accidentally is either beneath our notice or more than human. Society is something that precedes the individual. Anyone who either cannot lead the common life or is so self-sufficient as not to need it, and therefore does not partake of society, is either a beast or a god.

But he is not a human in the classical or traditional understanding of man. *This is an important shift in man's understanding of himself!*

According to Hobbes, it is because of the equality of persons and the quarrels and other unpleasantries and dangers associated with living in a *State of Nature*, that men need a common power to keep them in *awe* or make them behave.

Otherwise, men would remain in a state of war—every man against every man!

[Stay with me, dear reader, I promise this is going somewhere...]

## LOCKE'S VERSION OF SOCIAL CONTRACT THEORY

One should recognize many elements and terms employed by Thomas Hobbes in Locke's Social Contract Theory, although he is clearly not as pessimistic with regards to the state of nature in general and human nature in particular, the basic concepts remain intact.

Locke's description of the state of nature, unlike Hobbes's, ain't that bad! One would hardly describe it as 'solitary, poor, nasty, brutish, and short.' Locke's state of nature is unstable in many respects, but is not the horribly dangerous place imagined by Hobbes.

In the state of nature, according to Locke, all men are *free, equal,* and *independent.* This does not necessarily lead to a state of war, as in the case of Hobbes, but is mostly inconvenient.

Locke's understanding of society, like Hobbes, is that man is an *individual among individuals* and not a *social being* like he had been understood to be throughout the history of pre-modern western thought. (Recall the quote from Aristotle above.)

While there is no government in the state of nature, there is a spontaneous political order of sorts according to Locke—men are subject to the *natural law,* which for Locke, is synonymous with God's law.

The Law of God can also be called the Law of Reason. We learn what the natural law is through the use of reason.

The laws of nature (God or reason) are normative and not descriptive—it describes how people ought to act, not how they act or would likely act if given the chance. It is rooted in his understanding of property rights and what we call the golden rule...

Locke uses the word 'property' to denote 'lives, liberties, and estates' (Transformed by Jefferson in the Declaration to 'life, liberty, and the pursuit of happiness').

In the State of Nature, men retain two great powers:

1 – To do whatsoever he thinks fit for the preservation of himself and others so long as it does not violate the law of nature.

2 – The power to punish crimes against the law of nature.

The obvious question here is why would anyone, being in a state of nature where they are absolute lord over their own person and property, equal to the greatest, and subject to no other person, give this up to join with others to create a government or commonwealth?

It is that because, according to Locke, not all men obey the natural law, thus making the enjoyment of one's property unsecure. (So Hobbes's description of men in a State of Nature is not completely undone in the case of Locke's theory, is it?)

Why is this the case?

Because the natural law is often forsaken for the sake of personal interests or biases.

The great and *chief end,* therefore, of men's uniting into commonwealths, and putting themselves under government, *is the preservation of their property*, to which in the state of nature there are many things wanting.

For this reason, people give up many liberties for a few well-defined securities which, according to Locke, should include at least these three:

> 1 – The establishment of known laws received through common consent to be the standard of right and wrong in the commonwealth.
>
> (Natural law is often forsaken for personal interests or biases—now everyone knows what is expected of them.)
>
> 2 – The establishment of an indifferent judge with the authority to determine all differences according to the established laws.
>
> (Impartial judgments are difficult because of personal interests or biases—now everyone knows to whom matters of differences are to be appealed.)
>
> 3 – One to back and support the sentence when right and give it due execution.

Locke summarizes the formation of civil society as follows:

> But though men, when they enter into society, give up the equality, liberty, and executive power they had in the state of nature, into the hands of the society, to be so far disposed of by the legislative, as the good of the society shall require; yet it being only with an intention in every one the better to preserve himself, his liberty and property; (for no rational creature can be supposed to change his condition with an intention to be worse) the power of the society, or legislative constituted by them, can never be supposed to extend farther, than the common good; but is obliged to secure every one's property, by providing against those three defects above mentioned, that made the state of nature so unsafe and uneasy.

This argument is made with certain restraints, both fixed by the constituents of the commonwealth and the law of nature.

These restraints are enumerated by Locke as follows:

> First, They are to govern by promulgated established laws, not to be varied in particular cases, but to have one rule for rich and poor, for the favourite at court, and the country man at plough.
>
> Secondly, These laws also ought to be designed for no other end ultimately, but the good of the people.
>
> Thirdly, They must not raise taxes on the property of the people, without the consent of the people, given by themselves, or their deputies. And this properly concerns only such governments where the legislative is always in being, or at least where the people have

not reserved any part of the legislative to deputies, to be from time to time chosen by themselves.

Fourthly, The legislative neither must nor can transfer the power of making laws to any body else, or place it any where, but where the people have.

So, what happens when the ruler or rulers go beyond their lawful authority and set themselves against the people of the commonwealth?

Whenever the legislators endeavour to take away, and destroy the property of the people, or to reduce them to slavery under arbitrary power, they put themselves into a state of war with the people, who are thereupon absolved from any farther obedience, and are left to the common refuge, which God hath provided for all men, against force and violence. Whensoever therefore the legislative shall transgress this fundamental rule of society; and either by ambition, fear, folly or corruption, endeavour to grasp themselves, or put into the hands of any other, an absolute power over the lives, liberties, and estates of the people; by this breach of trust they forfeit the power the people had put into their hands for quite contrary ends, and it devolves to the people, who have a right to resume their original liberty, and, by the establishment of a new legislative, (such as they shall think fit) provide for their own safety and security, which is the end for which they are in society.

Who shall be the judge of whether or not the government is guilty of tyranny or usurpation of power?

The Supreme Court? Nope.

According to Locke:

> The people shall be judge; for who shall be judge whether his trustee or deputy acts well, and according to the trust reposed in him, but he who deputes him, and must, by having deputed him, have still a power to discard him, when he fails in his trust?

The people, after all, made the compact and set the conditions of the political incorporation called the state or commonwealth; the government is merely an agent of the people—created to represent their interests in certain enumerated cases. The government is the creature or product of the compact, not the originator of it.

## THE PROPOSITION IN CONTEXT

The important reason for discussing Hobbes is his description of the state of nature, common to both Hobbes and Locke's philosophy, and (as a curiosity at least) to show Hobbes's understanding of 'equality,' how it leads to a state of war. I have also included both philosophers to contrast their very different conclusions despite the fact that they both ground their argument for governmental legitimacy *via* the Social Contract as a means of correcting the deficiencies, inconvenience, and even dangers intendent in a state of nature. Hobbes' solution is an all-powerful form of governmental absolutism and Locke provides a more democratic solution.

These differences are not that of temperament: Hobbes, the misanthropic pessimist versus Locke, the enlightenment-era optimist. They are more fundamental—what is man? Is he fallen and debased by nature, or is he perfectible and can progress towards this perfection given the right set of circumstances? (An issue that still plagues us today!)

Regardless of these weighty metaphysical matters, I think we can understand why Jefferson was tempted to employ pieces of Locke's version of the Social Contract as a theoretical justification for independence—it 'fit' the narrative in certain respects—but the case for American independence did not really need a theoretical justification of a general nature unless it was for rhetorical purposes.

As far as arguments go, arguing from a general case to a specific case is considered to be deductive and, hence, an extremely strong form of argument. If it were universally true (as in the case of Locke) that men are created equal in the state of nature, create a commonwealth for their safety and happiness, and may alter or abolish it under certain conditions which are determined by themselves and no one else—no king, no court, no judge—then it is true in the case of British Americans.

The plain facts were enough, since the issue was between inherited and understood rights and privileges of Englishmen and a King who violated these rights and privileges. All of the enlightenment lingo may have provided a stronger argument (rhetorically speaking), but in time only served to confuse the people because they only remember the general part of the argument for independence and forget the specific reasons for independence and, at a later date, the form of government each former colony would, in fact, freely assume outside of the British realm.

To return to the proposition and the passage from whence it came, it seems clear that the only reason it was included is because it provided a litmus test to determine governmental legitimacy, namely, the consent of the governed. The 'all men are created equal' phrase refers to a condition in the state of nature, not a goal to be realised—in fact, it is one of the reasons for wanting to form governments.

Let us now return and re-read the passage and the proposition as it was understood by Jefferson in light of his use of Lockean Social Contract theory:

> We hold these Truths to be self-evident, that all Men are created equal [in a state of nature], that they are endowed by their Creator [in this state of nature] with certain unalienable Rights, that among these are Life,

Liberty, and the Pursuit of Happiness—That to secure these Rights, Governments are instituted among Men [through the Social Contract], deriving their just Powers from the Consent of the Governed [those who delegated a portion of their absolute liberty that they had in the state of nature to a governing apparatus for specific ends—safety or commodious living, for example, but in all cases that their lives might be better as a result of this contract...], that whenever any Form of Government becomes destructive of these Ends [as determined by the people who agreed to the specific terms of the contract] , it is the Right of the People to alter or to abolish it [fix it or dissolve it], and to institute new Government [which they believe to be more likely to fulfill its ends], laying its Foundation on such Principles, and organizing its Powers in such Form, as to them [and not the governing apparatus, which was created by a contract] shall seem most likely to effect their Safety and Happiness.

As far as I can tell, the only reason this passage was included (besides rhetorical strength), was that it provided a kind of test for determining legitimate political authority. It is determined not by equality or some other abstract principle, it was derived and only derived from THE CONSENT OF THE GOVERNED.

Why Lincoln chose to zero in on 'all men are created equal' when the entire point of the passage was not equality per se (as this was a characteristic of 'the state of nature' and part of the motivation to create a commonwealth), but where governments derive their power, is an interesting question.

Why does he state emphatically that 'all men were created equal' when he did not think that they were? This is true not only in matters of race—it is generally known by people who actually read what Lincoln said before and during the war—but also of

163

existing and (by that time) organic communities, made up 'of the people' of those communities (in our case, States) who judged for themselves and did so through what was then considered to be the avenue through which to ascertain and execute the desire or will of the people regarding specific issues related to laws and political relationships—a convention of the people.

What people? The very same government that acceded to and seceded from the first American Constitution, The Articles of Confederation (a perpetual union that turned out to be very short lived), in order to accede to (or not, according to the will of the people) the new Constitution of 1787—could not exercise the same authority as they had previously when the first Constitution was rejected and the new Constitution accepted? Apparently, Mr. Lincoln, who never acknowledged that the Southern States were ever out of the Union, thought it good policy to subjugate one part of the country to save a government? Not a national government— there was no such thing—but his imaginary government. What he called 'the national authority.'

The irony that in Lincoln's use of the Declaration of Independence in his defence of maintaining an 'indivisible' Union is almost too much to be true.

The whole document argues against Lincoln's understanding of the union, the source of legitimacy, and the plain facts of history as enumerated in this book, especially—and this is the long and short of it—that there never was and never has been a national form of government, at least one that could pass the test of legitimacy provided by Jefferson (by way of Locke) in the opening passages of the Declaration of Independence.

# About the Author

**PAUL C. GRAHAM** is the co-founder, co-owner, and Managing Director of Shotwell Publishing. His writings have appeared in several publications including the *Simms Review*, Abbeville Institute, and Reckonin.com. He has also appeared on CBS Nightly News, the BBC, NPR, AP, The Daily Ledger, The Mike Church Show, and several state and local news and talk outlets to discuss Southern history, culture, and symbols and why they should be preserved.

Graham is past president and Fellow of the South Carolina Masonic Research Society and the former editor of *The Palmetto Partisan (SC SCV)*.

He is a contributing author to *Understanding the War Between the States* (Society of Independent Southern Historians, 2015), *American History for Home Schools, 1607 to 1885* (Society of Independent Southern Historians, 2018), and *The Southern Tradition* (Abbeville Institute Press, 2019), editor of a collection of accounts from the South Carolina Slave Narratives entitled *When the Yankees Come: Former South Carolina Slaves Remember Sherman's Invasion* (2016), [Later updated and expanded in *When the Yankees Come: Former Carolina Slaves Remember Sherman's March FROM the Sea* (Shotwell Publishing, LLC, 2021)], and author of *Confederaphobia: An American Epidemic* (2017).

A native South Carolinian, Graham holds both a bachelor's and master's degree in philosophy from the University of South Carolina and taught this subject at the college level for over a decade.

He lives near old Saxe Gotha, South Carolina, with his beautiful bride of over 25 years, Suzette, together with their pets Mausie the dog and Oskar the cat.

# Latest Releases & Best Sellers

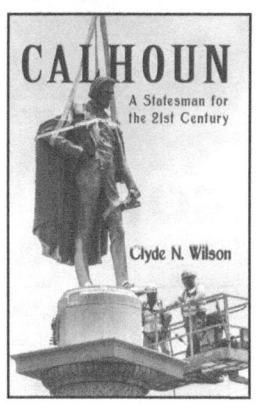

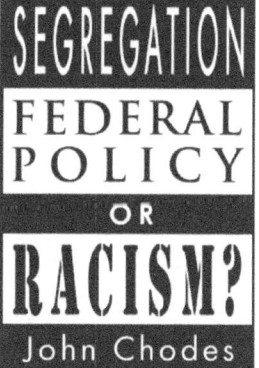

Made in United States
Cleveland, OH
05 June 2025

17518913R00105